Pub Walks in Wirral

The Wheatsheaf Inn, Raby (Walk 10)

Pub walks in
Wirral

*Superb circular walks
centered on some of Wirral's finest
country pubs*

Carl Rogers

MARA BOOKS

www.northerneyebooks.co.uk

First published in August 2025 by: **Mara Books**, 22 Crosland Terrace, Helsby, Frodsham, Cheshire, WA6 9LY.

All enquiries regarding sales telephone: (01928) 723744.

ISBN 978-1-902512-48-8

Printed and bound in the UK by 4Edge.

British Library Cataloguing-in-publication data.
A catalogue for this book is available from the British Library.

Whilst every effort has been made to ensure that the information contained in this book is correct, the author or the publisher can accept no responsibility for errors, loss or injury, however caused.

Maps based on out of copyright Ordnance Survey mapping.

Contents

A map of Wirral and location of the walks

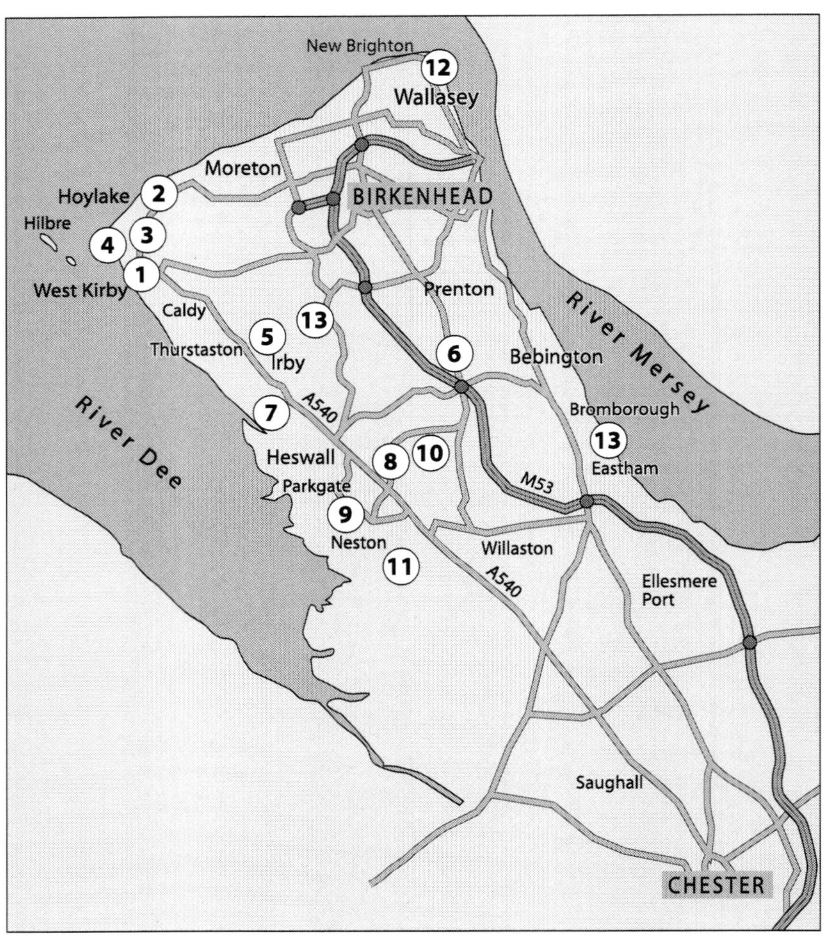

Introduction

WIRRAL OFFERS a uniquely satisfying experience for lovers of gentle, countryside walking and pubs full of character. With its mix of open marshes, woodlands, rolling fields and even stretches of sandy beach, it's a walker's paradise. And what better way to end a walk than with the promise of a welcoming pub.

Whether you're meandering along the Dee Estuary with sweeping views across to North Wales or winding through the leafy lanes around Raby and Thornton Hough, the landscape is rich in variety. And Wirral's pubs are as diverse as its terrain. For those who love a traditional, no-frills local, the Plasterers Arms in Hoylake is a gem. With its low ceilings, roaring log fire and friendly regulars, it's the kind of place where muddy boots are welcome and the ale is always well kept.

At the other end of the spectrum, The Red Fox near Thornton Hough offers a more refined experience. Housed in a tastefully restored period building, it blends heritage charm with modern elegance. Here, you'll find gourmet dining that doesn't compromise on warmth or authenticity—perfect for those who want to pair their walk with a touch of indulgence.

Speaking of ales, Wirral is a haven for real ale enthusiasts. Many pubs proudly serve local brews from microbreweries like Brimstage, Glen Affric and Peerless, offering everything from crisp golden ales to rich, malty stouts. Whether you're sipping a pint in a snug corner or enjoying a beer garden with views of the countryside, there's a sense of place in every glass.

In short, pub walks on the Wirral are more than just exercise—they're a celebration of local culture, culinary craft and the area's natural beauty. So lace up your boots, pick a walk and head out with the prospect of good food, great ale and warm hospitality.

Wirral real ale and breweries

by Rob Carter Editor of Camera's 'WirrAle Drinker'
www.wirrale.camara.org.uk

A brief history of Wirral's breweries: In the late 1800s and early 1900s Wirral had several commercial brewing operations but none have survived. The Argyle Brewery was founded as early as 1839 in Oxton Road Birkenhead and Anchor Brewery was founded in 1845 and based in Cleveland Street, Birkenhead. They merged in 1865 to form the Birkenhead Amalgamated Brewery which later became the Birkenhead Brewery Company Limited. This was ultimately taken over by Whitbread in 1967. The Wallasey Vale Brewery was founded in 1839 and operated by Spagg & Co supplying pubs in Wallasey until it was acquired by Liverpool based Higsons in 1919. West Cheshire Brewery had a site in Tranmere operating from 1864 before a succession of takeovers resulted in it being bought by Whitbread in 1967 and demolished to make way for housing. There was also the Grosvenor Brewery in Seacombe and the Yates Castle Brewery in Hamilton Street Birkenhead which, along with four breweries in Neston, were operating in the 1800s but were closed by 1900.

These days a large number of Wirral's pubs are owned and operated by Greene King so it is little surprise that the most common beers you are likely to encounter on the pumps in Wirral's pubs is Greene King IPA and Abbott Ale. However, the good news is, currently, there are four local breweries operating in Wirral.

Brimstage Brewery was founded in 2006 by Neil Young marking a return to commercial brewing in Wirral after a gap of nearly fourty years. The brewery is in a former farm outbuilding at Home Farm in Brimstage. Ownership of the brewery has since passed to his sons. The brewery mainly produces cask beer and nearly all of it is sold across Wirral within 10 miles of the brewery. The flagship beer is Trappers Hat, a pale session bitter which

accounts for much of the breweries' output. Other beers include Scarecrow bitter and Oystercatcher stout.
www.brimstagebrewery.com

Peerless Brewing was established in 2009 by Steve Briscoe in Pool Street, Birkenhead. The opening of the brewery saw a return to brewing in the town which had ceased in 1968 with the closure of Birkenhead Brewery. The name Peerless takes inspiration from the strap line of Birkenhead Brewery "Peerless Ales and Stouts". The brewery predominantly produces cask beer and supplies pubs across Wirral and beyond. Beers include Triple Blonde, a hoppy pale beer; Full Whack, a rich strong golden ale and Oatmeal Stout.
www.peerlessbrewing.co.uk

Glen Affric Brewery started production in 2016, established by brothers Craig and Callum McCormick in the Lightbox, Birkenhead close to the flyover. Initially all of the beer produced was sold in the onsite taproom. However, production has increased and they are now the largest brewing operation in Wirral supplying local pubs as well as distributing across the UK. Their focus is very much on keg beer but in 2023 they also started production of cask ales. The brewery produces a large number of different beers, a large majority being West Coast style IPAs with large amounts of hops added to impart citrus flavours. Beers you might see from Glen Affric include Highland Suntan, a citrus pale ale; Bevvie Across the Mersey, a session IPA and I Can't Believe it's Not-Ella, a chocolate and hazelnut porter.
www.glenaffricbrewery.com

Brooks Brewhouse is Wirral's latest and smallest brewery, situated in Hoylake. Founder Rob Brooks began producing beer as a hobby but became professional in 2017. He supplies a small number of pubs locally. All of the beers produced are un-fined meaning no chemicals have been added to remove the brewers yeast and hops in the beer after the brewing process so the beers are hazy when served. This also means they are suitable for vegans. The beers include Jai Ho IPA, Hopyard Bitter and Liverpool Porter.

www.brooks-brewhouse.co.uk

You will also commonly find beers in Wirral's pubs from breweries from neighbouring regions. For example: Neptune, Liverpool Brewing Co, Big Bog and Rock the Boat from Liverpool, along with Purple Moose, Conwy and Big Hand from North Wales, Weetwood from Kelsall, Coach House from Warrington and Spitting Feathers from Waverton.

With an increase in the number of freehouses on Wirral in recent years there is a wide range of beer to be found. So get your walking boots on and discover them!

The Walks

Village Road, West Kirby CH48 7HE

Tel: (0151) 541 6966 | **website:** www.ring-o-bells.co.uk

Brewery: Stange & Co Ltd (www.stangeandco.co.uk)

Opening times

Monday - Saturday	Noon - 11.00 pm
Sunday	Noon - 10.30 pm

Meal times

Monday - Saturday	Noon - 9.00 pm
Sunday	Noon - 6.00 pm

The pub

The **Ring O' Bells** is a recent addition to the expanding portfolio of Stange & Co Ltd, a local mini chain based in Parkgate at the Ship Inn (see walk 9). It opened in 2023 after extensive renovations aimed at returning it to it's Victorian origins. The result is a large, multi-room luxurious interior with a strong period feel, very much in the style of Stange & Co's other pubs. There are comfortable arm chairs, ideal for a restful pint, as well as large dinging areas and an extensive outside terrace.

An excellent range of cask beers are on offer from a wide range of breweries, including regulars from local Brimstage Brewery, Spitting Feathers and Glen Affric. Menus can be viewed and bookings made online.The pub is situated towards the end of the walk leaving an easy amble along the Wirral Way to return to the car park.

◆

The walk

Distance: 8½ miles/13.5km | **Allow:** 3½ hours

Start: Wirral Country Park car park in Croft Drive, Caldy. Free, no time restriction

OS Grid Ref: SJ 223 850 | **What3Words:** bloom.himself.sprawls

The route

1. From the car park head north (right-wards) along the Wirral Way (towards West Kirby).

Immediately before the first bridge, turn right up steps to the road. Go left and left again along 'Sandy Lane'. Before you reach the sea front, the road swings right just before the sailing club. Keep ahead here along 'South Parade' soon reaching the Marine Lake, used by the sailing club.

Except at high tide, the footpath around the seaward edge of the Marine Lake can be walked. It will be obvious if this isn't possible, so either follow the path around the lake or bear right along the waterfront.

The Marine Lake was opened way back in 1899 in an attempt to retain a sea front for West Kirby as the River Dee's deep water retreated leaving West Kirby high and dry. Originally used for salt water bath-

ing solving the problem of accessing the sea at low tide, the lake is now used mainly by the local sailing club.

At the end of the Marine Lake, bear left on to the little beach area in front of the café. The path ahead is straight forward. Beyond the beach it passes between saltmarsh on the seaward side and the low sand dunes to the right.

2. In around 800 metres there is a King Charles III England Coast

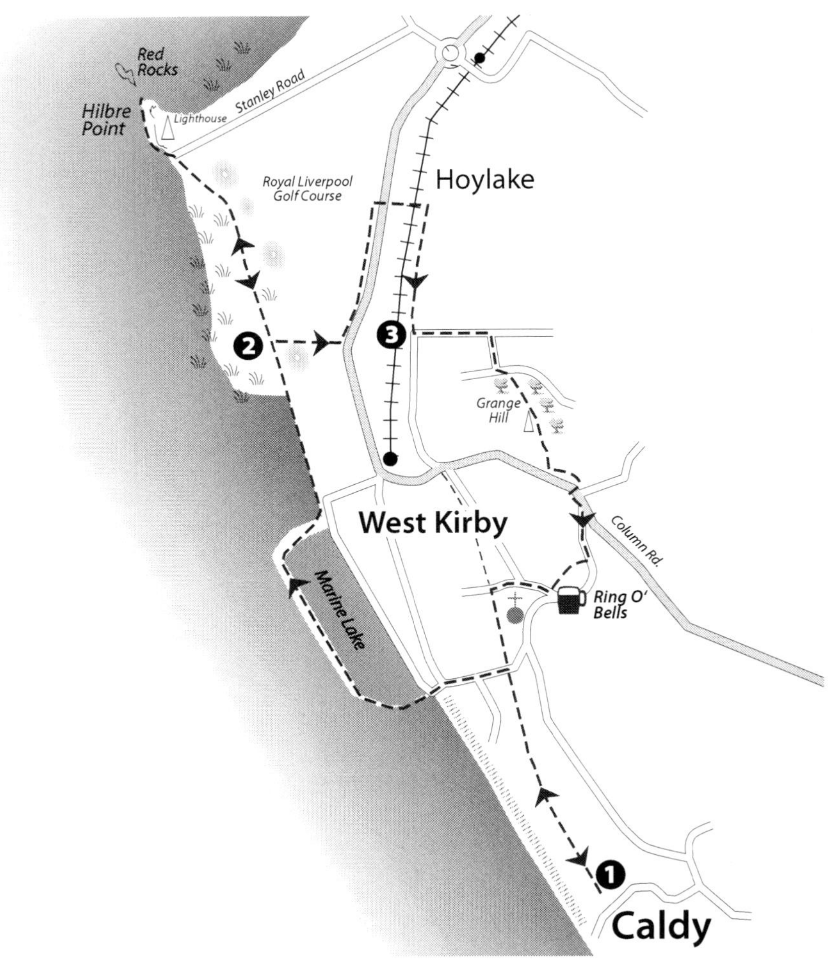

Following the path towards Hilbre Point

Path sign. The route goes right here up the steps, but it's worth continuing along the shoreline path between the dunes and the salt marsh to Hilbre Point for the views out to sea and along the North Wales coast. Retun to this point to continue the walk.

The reedbeds, salt marsh and dunes are included in the Red Rocks Nature Reserve, a coastal haven for several wildlife species including Wirral's only breeding colony of rare natterjack toads. Managed by Cheshire Wildlife Trust, the site supports diverse birdlife and over 50 flowering plant species, offering stunning views year-round.

At the top of the steps/dunes go through the kissing gate onto the golf course. Take a direct line across the fairway to a second kissing gate that leads into a short access road (Pinfold Lane). Go ahead along the road to reach the main road between Hoylake and West Kirby.

Turn left along the road and in around 700m, with 'Barn Hey' on the left, cross over and take the signed public footpath between high brick walls. This leads to the railway and a level

One of the few stretches of fine sand left on the Dee coast of the Wirral can be found at Hilbre Point

crossing. It goes without saying that caution is needed as trains are frequent and there is no warning as they approach. Beyond the railway you join a cyclway that runs parallel to the lines. Turn right along the cycleway.

3. At the end of the cycleway by 'West Kirby Sports Facility', turn left along the road. In around 350 metres, opposite the entrance to 'Next Game West Kirby', cross over and turn right into 'Birkett Road'. Follow 'Birkett Road' to the T junction and bear diagonally left across the road taking the footpath into the trees.

This is Grange Hill, a small pocket of open woodland and heath with wide views. Take the most obvious footpath ahead (ignore a left at a fork) towards the monument which soon becomes visible through the trees ahead.

The large monument on the summit of the hill is a memorial to the casualties of the two world wars. It has commanding views to the west, north and east — from the mouth of the River Dee to the Great Orme and the distant hills of Snowdonia, across northern Wirral to the Liverpool skyline. In very clear conditions the view extends all the way to the Cumbrian hills, over 70 miles away.

Continue on the surfaced footpath on the left side of the memorial to soon join a fenced footpath which bends right along the edge of gardens and above the road. At the end of the path bear left along the road (Grange Old Road) passing the Hoylake and West Kirby Sea Cadets.

At the T junction go right crossing over the main road and turn left along the pavement. In around 100m bear right along 'Village Road'. Pass 'Abbey Road' on the right and in about 50m take the signed footpath on the right between gardens. At the road turn left for the **Ring 'O Bells**.

From the Ring o' Bells turn right, then right again, soon passing Saint Bridget's Church on the left. Immediately before the old railway bridge, turn left down steps to join the Wirral Way. Turn left and follow the Wirral Way back to the car park to complete the walk.

West Kirby traces its roots back to Viking settlers who came here from Ireland in the 10th century. Its name means 'western village of the church'. There has been a church on the site of St Bridget's Church for over a thousand years. The town grew around this ancient parish, slightly inland from the modern town. Coastal locations were more vulnerable, the settlement later shifting toward the railway station during the Victorian era.

2. PLASTERS ARMS, HOYLAKE

35 Back Sea View, Hoylake, Wirral CH47 2DJ

Tel: 07546 327101 | **website:** currently no website

Brewery: Free House

Opening times

Monday - Saturday	Noon - 11.00 pm
Sunday	Noon - 10.30 pm

Meal times

Monday - Wednesday	No Service
Thursday & Friday	5pm - 9pm
Saturday	Noon - 9pm
Sunday	Noon - 6pm

The pub

The **Plasterers Arms** is very much a traditional locals pub with a strong community feel serving high quality cask ales. Originally part of an old fishing community, it's said to have been recorded in the 1751 census and may have once operated as the *Life Boat Inn* under Robert Little. Today, it retains its vintage charm with quirky décor, including a mirrored ceiling and displays of local history. Just 150 metres from the beach, it's a favourite among walkers and birdwatchers as well as locals.

The pub offers a warm, welcoming atmosphere with a snug bar and a larger lounge, plus an extended outdoor seating area. It serves a rotating selection of cask ales, including Purple Moose's Glaslyn Ale and Wantsum's 1381 Session Blond. Regular entertainment, quiz nights and friendly staff make it a beloved community hub. It was named Wirral CAMRA's Pub of the Season in Spring 2025.

The walk

Distance: 3¾ miles/6km | **Allow:** 1-1½ hours

Start: Park & Ride car park, Carr Lane, Hoylake. Free, no time restriction

OS Grid Ref: SJ 217 887 | **What3Words:** grub.mock.workers

The route

1. Take the cycleway that leaves the car park in the far right corner and runs parallel to the railway. In around 700m there is a signed public footpath crossing the railway on the right by a level crossing. Cross the railway here. It goes without saying that you should take extra care here, trains are frequent and there is no warning as they approach.

Beyond the railway the path continues between high brick walls to reach the main road (A553). Cross over and turn left along the pavement.

In around 700m, turn right into 'Pinfold Lane', a short access road between houses. At the end of the road a kissing gate leads onto the golf course. The right of way takes a direct line across the fairway to a kissing gate in the sand dunes above the shore.

The Royal Liverpool Golf Club, recently played host to the 151st Golf Open in 2023. It was opened in 1869 on what was then an area of exposed sand dunes making it one of the oldest golf courses in the country.

2. Go through the kissing gate and down the steps onto the King Charles III England Coast Path. Turn right and follow the sandy path between the sand dunes and the mashy shoreline towards Hilbre Point where the lighthouse is visible ahead.

The path bears left onto the beach at Hilbre Point. Follow the edge of the beach past the slipway and continue round to the right towards Hoylake Beach. Other than at high tide the beach can be walked all the way to Hoylake quite easily.

(If this isn't possible, or you have any doubts about the tide, turn right up the slipway into 'Stanley Road' and follow it to the junction with 'King's Gap'. Turn left and follow the road down to the sea front.)

In the last few years marsh grass has spread along this part of the coast degrading what was once a fine sandy beach. The sands are always on the move however, and occasionally uncover what is known as the 'submerged forest' — the remains of hundreds of trees, submerged during sea level rises since the end of the last Ice Age.

The sumerged forest, Meols

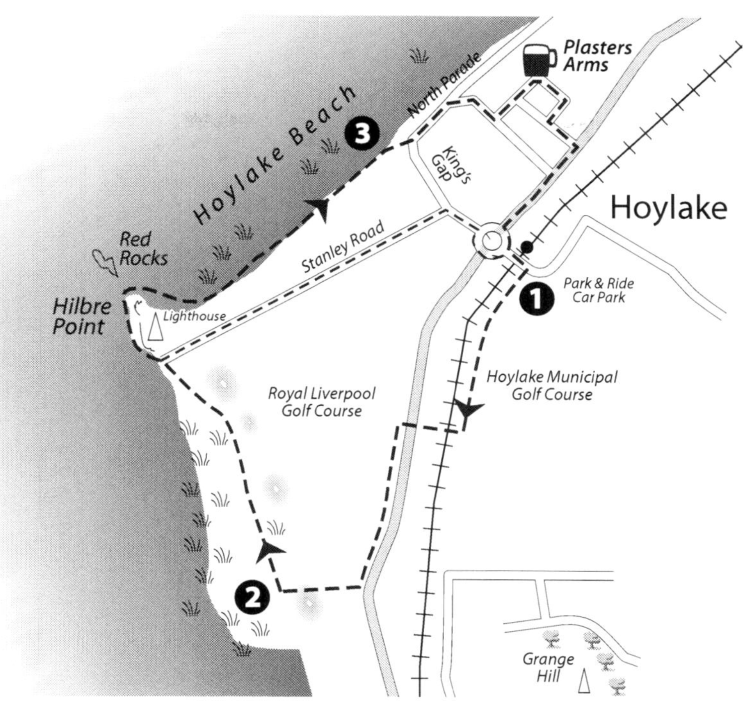

The forest has now disappeared, its last remains buried by sand over 50 years ago, although traces do appear occasionally. Many of Wirral's notable writers make mention of it and it was noted by William Webb as early as 1622.

In his book 'The Wirral Peninsula', the late Norman Ellison describes the forest as it appeared during the 1930s in this way: 'The clean stretch of sand was broken by a black patch, perhaps a half-mile in length, which a closer inspection revealed to be a thick stratum of peat, brown twigs, leaves, mosses, ferns and lichens, all tightly compressed. Above this mass, a large number of tree trunks, perhaps three or four feet high, stood erect, whilst many fallen trunks and large branches lay partly buried.'

This bizarre 'forest' seems to have been the result of inundation by the sea into an area of ancient woodland before the clearances of the Middle Ages—possibly the erosion or collapse of sheltering sand dunes which have now completely disappeared. The coastline is an area of constant change and the area of north Wirral is known to have undergone considerable change in fairly recent times.

One of the hardest puzzles to solve regarding the forest is not its existence, but the vast quantity of antiquities which have been discovered there. In all over 5,000 objects have been recorded with an interval of around 1,700 years between the earliest and latest finds. These include Saxon, Greek and Roman coins, spurs, daggers, swords, keys, buckles, brooches, harnesses and many other items too numerous to mention. Even with the existence of the anchorage at nearby Hoyle Lake and the Roman outpost which is thought to have existed at Meols, it is still difficult to explain how such vast quantities of objects with such a large time span came to be gathered together in so small an area.

Continue along the beach to 'North Parade'. Keep to the edge of the marshes close to the sea wall where a footpath is developing. (If you need to get off the beach, an access path into 'Beach Road'—about halfway between Hilbre Point and North Parade—leads onto 'Stanley Road'.)

3. Go ahead along 'North Parade' (the road along the sea front, or follow the emerging footpath along the grassy upper edge of the beach. In around 200m bear right into 'Alderley Road'. At 'Grove Place' turn left and follow the road to the **Plasters Arms**.

Leaving the Plasters Arms, turn left and at the T junction go right. At the end of 'Grove Road' turn left into 'Lake Place'. Continue to the end of 'Lake Place' to reach the main road in Hoylake and turn right.

Follow the road through Hoylake to the roundabout. Turn left here along 'Carr Lane'. Follow Carr Lane to the Park & Ride car park just beyond the level crossing to complete the walk.

3. THE WHITE LION, WEST KIRBY

51 Grange Road, West Kirby CH48 4EE

Tel: (0151) 625 9037 | **website:** whitelionwestkirby.co.uk

Brewery: Free House

Opening times

Monday - Saturday	Noon - 11.00 pm
Sunday	Noon - 10.30 pm

Meal times

Monday - Wednesday	No Service
Thursday & Friday	5pm - 9pm
Saturday	Noon - 9pm
Sunday	Noon - 6pm

The pub

The White Lion is a historic sandstone pub nestled in the heart of West Kirby dating back over 200 years. Renowned for its cosy atmosphere, it features a log burner, comfortable seating, spacious beer garden and fish pond.

The pub offers five well-kept cask ales, is Cask Marque accredited, and proudly appears in the CAMRA Good Beer Guide. A massive wooden conservatory adds charm and warmth, making it a favourite spot year-round. The White Lion is dog-friendly both inside and out, and serves food from Bamboo Thai, blending traditional pub culture with vibrant cuisine.

◆

The walk

Distance: 4¾ miles/7.5km | **Allow:** 1½–2 hours

Start: Wirral Country Park car park in Croft Drive, Caldy. Free, no time restriction

OS Grid Ref: SJ 223 850 | **What3Words:** constrain.clipped.decompose

The route

1. Walk back to the car park entrance and turn left along 'Croft Drive'. In about 200m, where the road swings to the right, bear left onto a signed bridleway. Follow the sandy path between large wooded gardens to reach the road in the centre of Caldy village opposite the church. Turn right and walk along the road.

The name Caldy has intriguing roots. It was recorded in the Domesday Book of 1086 as Calders, an Old English term likely derived from cald-ears, meaning "cold hill" or, more colorfully, "cold arse" — a reference to the prominent, exposed hill on which Caldy and Grange sit. The spelling evolved over time, appearing as Caldei in 1182 and Cawedy by 1606. This distinctive etymology reflects both the landscape and the linguistic quirks of Anglo-Saxon place-naming.

Follow the road as is curves past the church and beside Caldy Manor. Continue for another 300m to the signed footpath on the left to 'Newton'. This is FP48 and is directly opposite a signed footpath to Thurstaston on the right. Turn left and follow the footpath into Stapledon Wood with gardens on the right at first.

After stone steps keep right beside the wall with fields beyond on the right.

Just over 100m after the steps go left at a fork and climb up through the woods passing a house and garden on the left to reach a road end on the left. Go half-right here (ignore the signed bridleway on the right) on a clear path through the woods that soon swings left. Keep to the main footpath soon with a fenced garden and large house on the left. Ignore a left fork keeping ahead to eventually go through a gap in a sandstone wall. Turn right onto a path between stone walls and in 10m or so turn left through a second gap in the wall. The footpath cuts through a tangle of rhodedendrons, soon reaching the edge of the woods where there is a cross paths junction.

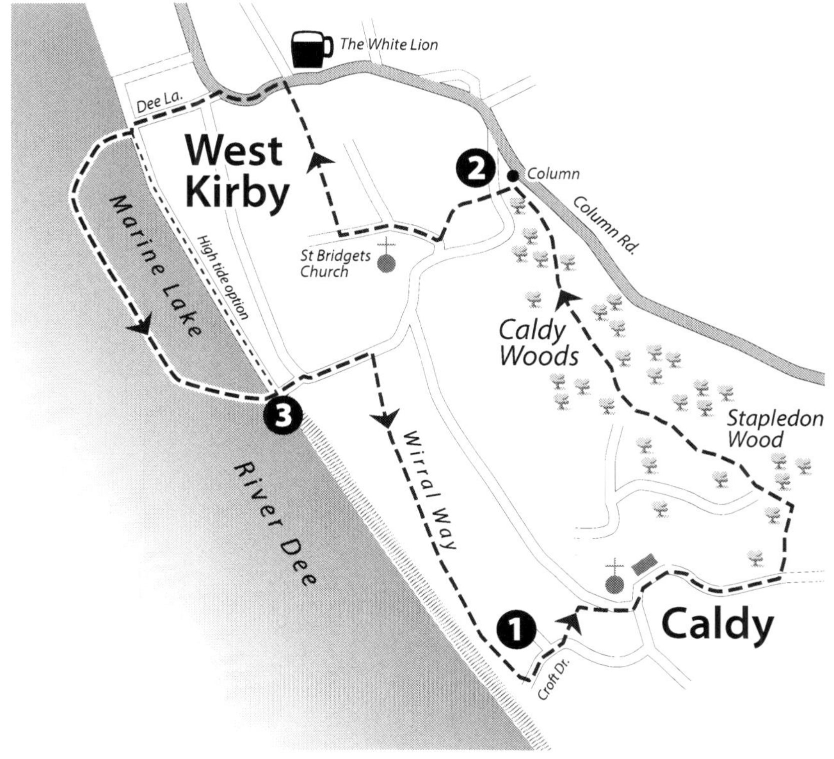

Caldy village

Take the footpath straight ahead passing through a more open area of young birch and heather. Keep on the main footpath directly ahead here to eventually reach the Alfred Vaughan Paton memorial and viewfinder.

This offers a wide view of the surrounding coast, from the Hilbre Islands to Flintshire, the Great Orme and distant Snowdonia.

Continue on the broad footpath beyond the viewfinder ignoring ajoining paths to reach a T junction. Bear right and continue, ignoring a left at a fork, until you reach the tall sandstone pillar know as The Beacon.

This well known Wirral landmark was erected in 1841 by the Trustees of Liverpool Docks as a beacon for river traffic and replaced a large windmill used for the same purpose, destroyed by gales two years previously. The large mill stone is presumably a relic from the mill.

2. Take the footpath which drops steeply down steps from the Beacon (to the left as you approached). Lower down steps lead onto the road. Cross over and take the footpath opposite contained between gardens. At the end of the path turn right and follow the road past St. Bridgets Church and Ashton Park. Continue to cross the old bridge over the Wirral Way. Look for the access path on the left after the bridge. Turn left here and left again under the bridge. Follow the Wirral Way to its end in the centre of West Kirby.

Turn right and **The White Lion** is about 100m along the road on the opposite side.

Leaving pub turn right and walk down through the centre of West Kirby. Turn left into 'Dee Lane' and walk past Morrisons to reach the waterfront, West Kirby beach and the Marine Lake. The footpath around the lake makes for a more enjoyable walk than the road so follow the narrow footpath between the lake and the sea. This can be walked at all but the highest tides. If you are in any doubt follow the road instead.

The Marine Lake was built in the closing years of the nineteenth century to retain a sea front for West Kirby as the River Dee's deep water channel moved from the Wirral side of the estuary over to the Welsh side. This followed the land reclamation schemes of the late 1700s which saw the River Dee moved into a canal-like channel and the building of seawalls right up to Burton Point.

Originally used for salt water bathing solving the problem of accessing the sea at low tide, the lake is now used mainly by the local sailing club.

3. At the end of the lake go straight ahead along the road past the sailing club and ahead again at the next junction. Follow the road over the Wirral Way bridge, turning right at 'York Avenue', then immediately right down onto the Wirral Way. Turn left and follow the Wirral Way back to the car park to complete the walk.

4. WEST KIRBY TAP, WEST KIRBY

Grange Road, West Kirby CH48 4DY

Tel: (0151) 625 0350 | **website**: www.westkirbytap.co.uk

Brewery: Spitting Feathers

Opening times
Monday - Sunday   Noon - 11.00 pm

Meal times
Monday - Tuesday   No Service
Wednesday & Friday   2pm - 9pm
Saturday   Noon - 9pm
Sunday   Noon - 7pm

The pub

The **West Kirby Tap** is a vibrant real ale tap bar located in the heart of West Kirby, just a short stroll from the beach. Part of the Spitting Feathers brewery family, it's known for its eclectic beer selection, cozy atmosphere and community spirit. Inside, you'll find a log burner, friendly staff and a welcoming vibe that makes it a favourite among both locals and visitors.

The pub features 8 hand pulls (7 cask ales and 1 cider), 4 keg lines, continental lagers and a wide array of bottled and canned craft beers. Its kitchen serves freshly made stone-baked pizzas and bar snacks daily, perfectly paired with the award-winning brews. Dog-friendly and often hosting live music, it's a popular spot for post-walk pints or relaxed evenings. With five consecutive entries in the *Good Beer Guide*, the West Kirby Tap continues to impress as a cornerstone of Wirral's craft beer scene.

The walk

Distance: 7¼ miles/11.5km | **Allow:** 2½-3 hours

Start: Park & Ride car park, Carr Lane, Hoylake. Free, no time restriction

OS Grid Ref: SJ 217 887 | **What3Words:** grub.mock.workers

The route

1. Take the cycleway that leaves the car park in the far right corner and runs parallel to the railway. In around 700m there is a signed public footpath crossing the railway on the right by a level crossing. Cross the railway here. It goes without saying that you should take extra care here, trains are frequent and there is no warning of an approaching train.

Beyond the railway the path continues between high brick walls to reach the road (A553). Cross over and turn left along the pavement.

In around 700m, turn right into 'Pinfold Lane', a short access road between houses. At the end of the road a kissing gate leads onto the golf course. The right of way takes a direct line across the fairway to a kissing gate in the sand dunes above the shore.

2. Descend the steps and turn left along the shoreline path to reach the beach front and café in West Kirby beside the Marine Lake. The only safe option for crossing to Hilbre starts from here.

Three islands make up the Hilbre group: Little Eye, Little Hilbre Island and Hilbre Island, arranged along a sandstone reef just over two kilometres long. Little Eye is the southern most (to the left of the three) and smallest of the islands; the island almost directly ahead as you look out from West Kirby beach front. The route heads for Little Eye first, a walk across the flat sands of just over 1km/¾ mile.

Little Eye is well named—a tiny clump of rough grass about the size of a golf putting green, sat on a much larger area of flat sandstone terrace. These sandstone formations were once part of the mainland, becoming islands as sea levels rose after the last Ice Age.

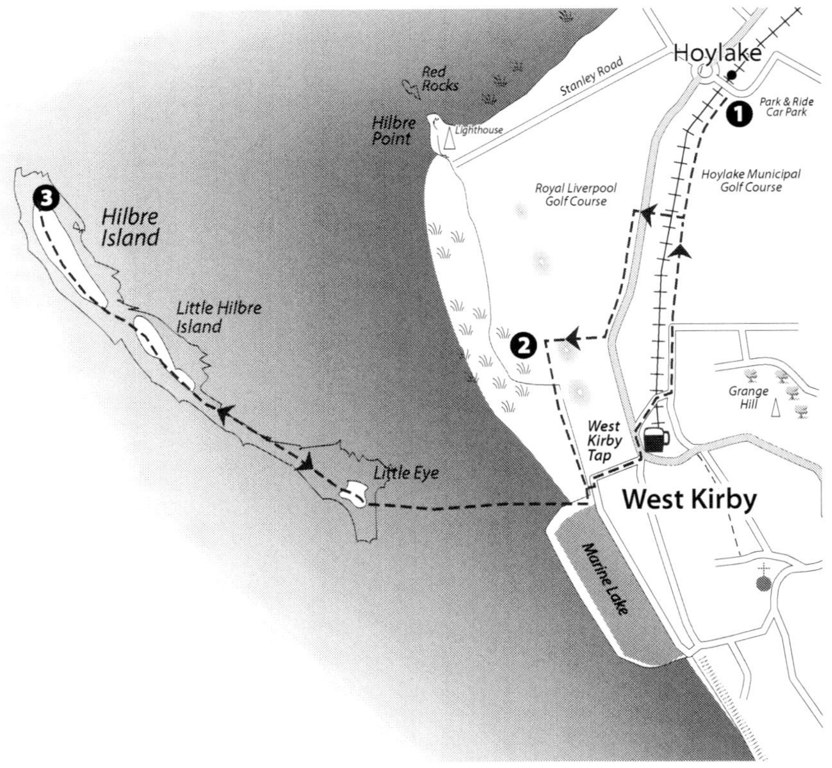

A sea arch on Hilbre Island

The way ahead is straightforward now and bears right along the sandstone rocks to Little Hilbre Island, another kilometre or so.

Little Hilbre is much larger than Little Eye—almost 350 metres long— and is ringed by small sandstone cliffs. The footpath heads up from a small sandy cove and along the grassy ridge, before more terraced sandstone leads eventually to Hilbre Island.

A 4x4 track leads up onto the island to the left of the little beach as you approach.

Human activity on Hilbre dates back to the Stone Age, with archaeological finds including Roman pottery and Bronze Age tools. In the medieval period, Hilbre became a religious site. A chapel dedicated to St. Hildeburgh (giving the islands their name) was built and by the 12th century, Benedictine monks from Chester Cathedral established a cell and church on the island. It became a place of pilgrimage and remnants of the chapel and fish ponds remain.

During the 18th century, Hilbre was associated with smuggling and pirate activity, taking advantage of its secluded coves. In the 19th century, a lifeboat station was built to aid shipwrecked sailors. The island also played a strategic role in both World Wars, with military installations guarding the coastline.

Today, Hilbre is a designated Local Nature Reserve, known for its rich birdlife, seals and marine biodiversity. It remains uninhabited, except for occasional researchers and visitors who walk across the sands at low tide to explore its unique blend of natural beauty and layered history.

A rough road and/or footpaths lead across the island to the far end where there are ruins of the old lifeboat station. There are half a dozen buildings on the island but no one lives here permenantly, despite the existence of at least one holiday home.

Looking towards Hilbre Island from Little Hilbre Island

Looking back to West Kirby from Hilbre Island

3. To return, retrace your steps back to Little Hilbre Island and Little Eye before heading back across the sands, following the outward route, back to West Kirby beach.

Back on dry land, walk ahead along 'Dee Lane' with Morrisons supermarket on the right. At the T junction at the end of the road, turn left and **West Kirby Tap** is on the far side of the road in around 100m or so.

Leaving the Tap, turn right and bear right in a few metres into 'Bridge Lane'. Follow 'Bridge Lane' over the railway and at the crossroads junction turn left. This is 'Greenbank Road'. Where the road bends sharp right in around 400m, bear left (ahead) through the little car park for 'West Kirby Sports Facility' and join the footpath and cycleway on the left which runs between the hockey pitch and railway. Follow this back to the car park to complete the walk.

Mill Lane, Greasby CH49 3NT

Tel: (0151) 678 0198 | **website:** irbymill.co.uk

Brewery: Free House

Opening times

Monday - Sunday   Noon - 11pm

Meal times

Monday - Sunday   Noon - 9pm

The pub

Irby Mill is a cosy country pub, built on the site of a former wind-mill. First opened in 1980, it blends rustic sandstone architecture with a warm, welcoming interior. Known for its award-winning selection of eight cask ales, Irby Mill features brews from local favourites like Peerless, Weetwood Ales and Rock the Boat. The pub is Cask Marque accredited and has earned CAMRA recognition for its ale quality.

Its menu showcases hearty, homecooked food using locally sourced ingredients—steaks from Bredbury Catering, sausages from Muffs of Bromborough and seasonal British vegetables. The beer garden is a popular spot in summer and the pub is dog-friendly both inside and out.

The walk

Distance: 8 miles/12.75km | **Allow:** 3–3½ hours

Start: Free car park for Thurstaston Hill on the A540, just beyond the Cottage Loaf pub

OS Grid Ref: SJ 246 845 | **What3Words:** chromatic.trickle.tragedy

The route

1. Leave the car park by the footpath at the far end. At a T junction turn right and continue to the main road. Bear left along the road passing the Cottage Loaf pub. Keep ahead at the roundabout along 'Telegraph Road' and just beyond the bus stop, cross over into 'Church Lane'.

Walk down the lane to Thurstaston church and old hall and turn left onto the signed footpath 'To Dungeon Wood'. The right of way follows a dirt track at first, then a hedged footpath between fields.

2. At a footpath junction adjacent to 'The Dungeon' woods, turn right and follow the footpath into the trees beside the stream. Cross a footbridge and continue above a small waterfall, then more steeply down to cross another footbridge at the bottom of the slope. A fenced footpath now leads between fields still beside the stream to join the Wirral Way. Turn right along the Wirral Way.

As you approach the the visitor centre car park, bear right off the old trackbed and walk out of the car park access to the café (Flissy's Coffee Shop) on the left (good opportunity for a mid-walk break). Turn left at the road T junction in front of the café and follow the road over the bridge and past the caravan site entrance. At the end of the road a footpath on the right leads down a series of wooden steps 'To the Beach'.

Turn right along the shore passing the curious Shore Cottage, once a customs house. The beach can be walked at most states of the tide but care should be taken with timing. Avoid a rising tide with less than two hours before high tide. (If tides are not favourable return to the Wirral Way and continue to Caldy where a railway bridge once carried the railway over the road.)

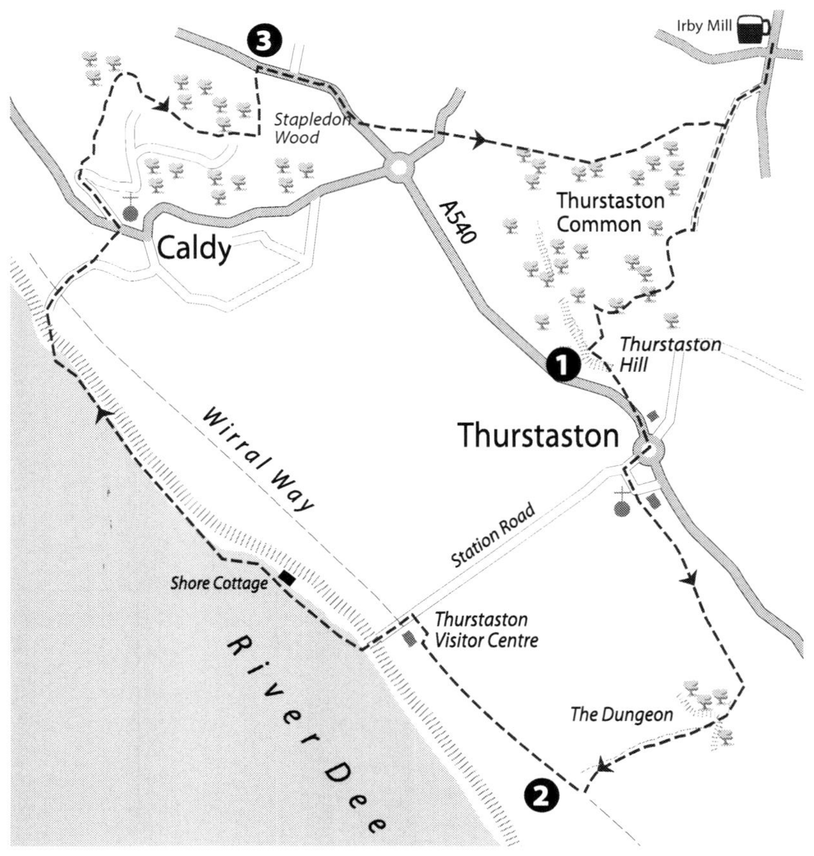

Shore Cottage

Ignore the first ramp off the beach in around 1km/¾ mile, continuing to the next beach access, just over 1km further on. (Again if you have any doubts about the tide, you can leave the beach here, following the road up past the golf club to join the Wirral Way.)

Turn right up the steps to the road end and follow the road past the Wirral Way where a bridge once carried the railway over the lane. (The tidal option joins here from the right.) Walk up the road and where this swings to the right take the sandy path between large gardens on the left (ahead). Follow this up to the road in the centre of Caldy village.

Turn left along the road for a few metres, then cross over and bear right up 'Kings Drive'. On the first sharp right-hand bend, take the signed footpath (55) on the left. In a few metres the path swings left through a gap in a sandstone wall. Don't go through the gap, instead take a path on the right, which shortly swings left up through old pines to a footpath T junction where there is

The summit of Thurstaston Hill

a low footpath marker post. Turn left here soon passing a section of stone wall with a house just visible on the right. Keep right at a fork here and ignore footpaths on the left, climbing to reach an open area with flat rocks, a seat on the right and wide views across West Kirby to Hilbre and North Wales.

Continue ahead on a good path with fenced/walled gardens occasionally visible over to the right. Ignore a fenced path between gardens on the right continuing ahead. At a larger clearing with bench seats, a cross paths junction and a large 'Footpaths Society' sign, turn right.

The footpath stays close to walled gardens on the right until the wall ends at a corner. Ignore a footpath immediately on the right keeping ahead for around 20m to a cross paths junction. Turn right here and follow the footpath through thicker woodland to eventually pass through a gap in a stone wall. Turn right along a broad path between stone walls for about 10m, then go left through a gap in the opposite wall. There is a fork in the path almost immediately—keep right. Follow this well worn footpath through the woods ignoring minor joining paths on either side. Eventually you will see a large house with fenced gardens on the right and in around 400m (from the gap in the wall), you will meet a road end with houses on the right.

Ignore the signed bridleway on the left continuing ahead with houses/gardens still on the right. Head down through the trees to meet a crossing footpath with fields ahead. Turn left along this footpath and follow it, never far from fields on the right, to reach the road.

3. Cross over and turn right. In around 700m, and after the house 'Beech Lea' turn left onto the signed public footpath. This is fenced/hedged on both sides and eventually meets the driveway to a gated cottage on the left. Go ahead along the drive to meet the road. Cross over and take the signed footpath (13) into the woods of Thurstaston Common.

At metal railings go through the kissing gate ahead and keep ahead beside the sandstone wall. At the end of the railings go through a gap in the wall and walk with the wall on your right. You will soon have to pass through the wall again and and walk with the wall on your left to reach a better path, but keep ahead still following the wall. The wall becomes intermittent but continue ahead and it will appear again here and there.

Soon you will see the large mock Tudor house of Hill Bark over to the left and a little further on, a large grass field beyond the wall on the left. Continue ahead.

After a second large grass field on the left, the path ahead drops to a footbridge in the corner of the common. Cross the footbridge, climb steps and follow the fenced footpath ahead (don't stray into 'Irby Quarry Meadows' on the left).

At a rough access road turn right and follow the road as it rises, then swings left to eventually reach the main road. Turn left to reach the **Irby Mill** pub.

From the pub, retrace your steps along 'Mill Hill Road' turning right into 'Sandy Lane North'. Pass houses on the right and where the road swings right, go straight ahead on the signed bridleway. At the far side of the woods you reach a road end. Take the signed footpath (51) on the right which will take you back into Thurstaston Common. Cross the wooden footbridge, turn left along the path and keep left at a fork.

After around 350m, go through a wooden kissing gate on the right. The woods soon thin out and there is a large field beyond the hedge on the right. Keep ahead eventually passing through a small gate beside a large farm gate to reach a broad unsurfaced access road. Turn right along the road and as you pass beneath overhead cables, turn sharp left onto a narrow footpath. Follow the path to reach a road end. Bear half-right here to reach a broad sandy footpath, then turn right almost immediately (red brick house on the left) onto a rising footpath. Follow this to the summit of Thurstaston Hill.

Thurstaston Common is the largest area of open heath and woodland in Wirral. From its summit dramatic views stretch across the Dee Estuary to the Welsh hills—both the Clwydian Range and, if you are lucky, the northern edge of Snowdonia—as well as south and east across Wirral to the distant Liverpool skyline. The Common is a haven for wildlife, with seasonal bursts of heather and gorse.

With your back to the Dee estuary, take the path that heads right and keep right at a fork to reach the car park to complete the walk.

Following the King Charles III England Coast Path near Parkgate (walk 9)

Approaching Hilbre Island (walk 4)

Fort Perch Rock, New Brighton (walk 12)

Grenville Collins' sea chart of the River Dee and Wirrral coast, 1693

A woodland footpath in Eastham Country Park (walk 13)

The Wheatsheaf Inn, Wirral's most iconic country pub (walk 10)

The summit of Thursaston Hill (walk 5)

Perch Rock Lighthouse, New Brighton (walk 12)

The tiny Little Eye, one of the Hilbre Islands (walk 4)

Storm waves on the sea front, Wallasey (walk 12)

Heather flourishes in Wirral's pockets of lowland Heath

The Wirral Way (walk 3)

The beach at Hilbre Point (walk 2)

6. TRAVELLERS REST, Higher Bebbington

169 Mount Road, Higher Bebbington CH63 8PJ

Tel: (0151) 608 2988 | **website**: thetravsbebington.co.uk

Brewery: Free House

Opening times
Monday - Thursday	Noon - 11pm
Friday & Saturday	Noon - 11pm
Sunday	Noon - 11pm

Meal times
Monday & Tuesday	Noon - 2pm
Wednesday & Thursday	Noon - 2pm, 5.30pm - 7.45pm
Friday & Saturday	Noon - 7.45pm
Sunday	Noon - 5.45pm

The pub

The **Travellers Rest** is a cherished 'locals' style pub known for its warm atmosphere and hearty fare. A former coaching inn, its origins trace back to the 19th century when it was operating as a public house under the Birkenhead Brewery. Decorated throughout with brasses and bric-a-brac, the main area has a central bar with two side rooms. Guest ales are often from local microbreweries like Brimstage and Peerless. One changing real cider. There is a quiz night on Monday along with is live music on Saturday.

Beyond its architectural and operational legacy, the pub gained renewed recognition during the COVID-19 pandemic. Landlord Keith Irving and his team were named 'lockdown heroes' by Wirral CAMRA for their inventive community support—offering takeaway cask ales, food deliveries and festive treats to keep spirits high and the business afloat.

◆

The walk

Distance: 6½ miles/10.5km | **Allow:** 2–2½ hours

Start: Layby in Marsh Lane, Bebbington. Free parking no time restriction

OS Grid Ref: SJ 313 851 | **What3Words:** fields.soon.future

The route

1. From the layby, walk down the lane to the lower end of the woods and turn left through the gate onto the broad woodland path. Following the line of an old tramway associated with the nearby quarries, this path heads directly though Storeton Wood.

At a crossing lane ('Rest Hill Road') go ahead into the next strip of woodland following a farm access track. Immediately before the farm, bear right onto a hedged footpath which emerges where the driveway to 'Hillside Cottages' meets a lane. Turn left up the lane to the main road.

2. At the top of 'Redhill Road', cross over and go through the gap in the wall (to the right of 'Bracken Lane'). Turn right now and

The path through Storeton Wood

follow a narrow footpath through the trees passing a car park on the left. The path continues along the edge of the golf course passing through a strip of woodland with the main road over to the right.

At a lane, cross over taking the signed footpath opposite. In around 20m bear right where the right of way splits, continuing around the edge of the golf course.

At the far end of the golf course, and just before fields ahead, the path bears right out of the trees to emerge on the road (B5137). Cross over, turn left, then right along 'Old Clatterbridge Road'.

Pass Claremont Farm Shop and café on the left. There is an excellent tearoom here if you fancy a break, otherwise continue along the lane eventually bearing right over the M53.

Continue to the main road and keep left along the footway. Keep beside the road until it dips to the bridge over Clatter Brook (Clatter Bridge). Cross over here opposite the entrance to Claire

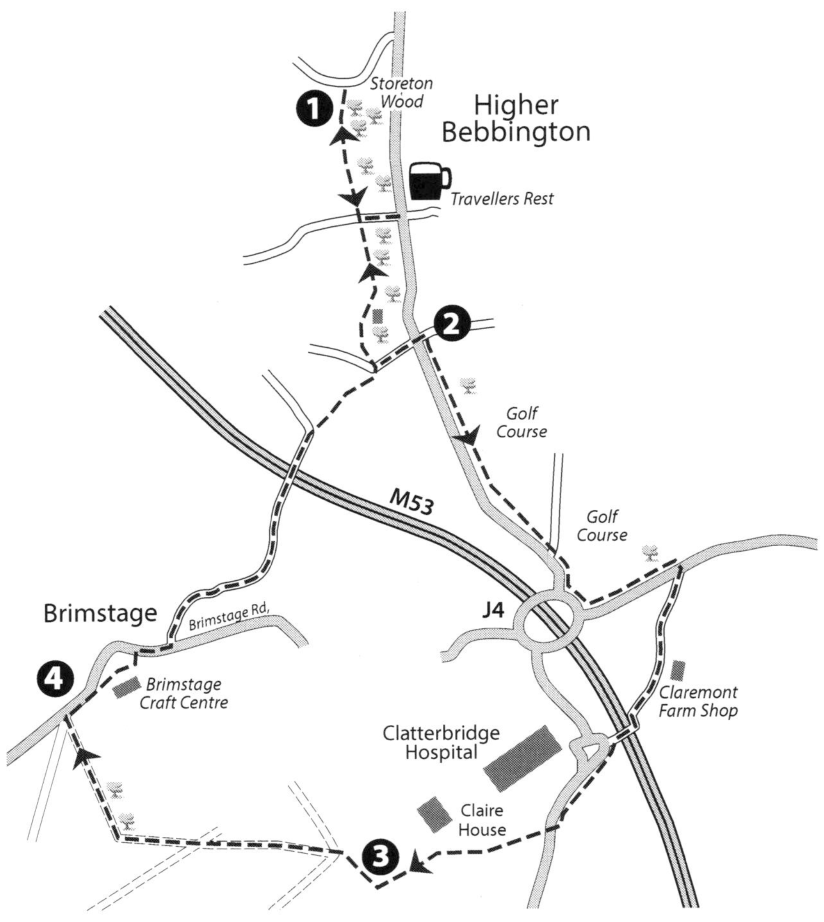

House. Take the signed footpath immediately to the left of the main gateway. Follow the fenced footpath beside the grounds to enter fields through a kissing gate. The path heads up the field edge to the top corner to join a farm track.

3. Turn right along the track. In around 400m this curves left to a junction of unsurfaced farm roads. Go straight ahead to follow the signed bridleway. This is contained by hedges and soon crosses an estate driveway. Keep ahead to eventually reach a T junction. Turn right here and follow the hedged bridleway to the road.

4. Turn right at the road ('Talbot Ave'), then right at the main road. Where the road swings to the left, take the signed footpath ahead which cuts across fields to enter the car park at Brimstage Craft Centre. Walk down the car park access road bearing left to the road. Turn right along the road, then cross over (in around 100m) and turn left down 'Brimstage Lane'.

Local brewers, Brimstage Brewery are based in the farm buildings on the right here.

Follow the lane passing under the motorway and on the bend, take the signed 'Public footpath to Higher Bebbington' ahead. The right of way takes a direct line through three small fields to enter an access road by a kissing gate. Turn left, then right along the lane. Almost immediately, turn left at the driveway to 'Hillside Cottages'. Take the footpath to the left of the driveway and retrace the outward route along the hedged path, then along the farm access road to reach the lane crossed at the beginning of the walk ('Rest Hill Road'). Turn right up the lane to reach the **Travellers Rest**.

Return to this point and retrace the outward route through Storeton Wood to complete the walk.

The woods were once the site of a sandstone quarry, supplying stone for major construction projects in Birkenhead and Liverpool. A tramline, designed by George Stephenson in 1837, ran through the woods to transport stone to Bromborough where it was loaded onto ships.

In 1838, quarrymen discovered fossilized footprints in the sandstone, later identified as belonging to 'Chirotherium', a crocodile-like creature from the Triassic period. The name means 'Hand Animal', from the hand-shaped prints found in the quarry walls.

The woods are currently maintained by the Woodland Trust and the Friends of Storeton Woods, preserving its ecological and historical value.

7. FOX & HOUNDS, BARNSTON

107 Barnston Road, Barnston CH61 1BW

Tel: (0151) 648 7685 | **website:** www.the-fox-hounds.co.uk

Brewery: Stange & Co Ltd (www.stangeandco.co.uk)

Opening times

Monday - Saturday	Noon - 11pm
Sunday	Noon - 10.30pm

Meal times

Monday - Sunday	Noon - 9pm

The pub

Built in 1910, but with roots stretching back nearly 400 years, the **Fox & Hounds** stands on one of the oldest pub sites in the region, originally serving farm labourers and weary travellers navigating the once treacherous 'Barnston dip'. Today, it, blends period charm with modern hospitality. Its cozy interiors feature open fires, a traditional bar room and bright garden rooms, creating a welcoming atmosphere year-round.

The menu showcases British pub classics alongside seasonal specials crafted from locally-sourced ingredients. Signature dishes include freshly battered fish and chips, hearty roasts, and gourmet burgers. The bar boasts local ales like Brimstage Brewery's Trapper's Hat, plus an impressive selection of whiskies, gins and wines.

The walk

Distance: 6 miles/9.5km | **Allow:** 2–2½ hours

Start: Free public car park in Riverbank Road, Heswall. No time restriction

OS Grid Ref: SJ 263 805 | **What3Words:** focal.fonts.healers

The route

1. Leave the car park at the far end where a footpath continues along what was at one time the sea front. The sandstone sea wall and metal railing recall a time when there was a beach here known as 'Heswall Shore' (see the photo on page 49). The ramp from the car park originally enabled bathers to get down onto the sand. Turn right along the marsh edge.

This can be wet for a short section where a stream crosses the path, but there are stepping stones. (If this section is too wet return to the car park, turn left up the road, follow it round to the left and continue to the end. Contiunue from point 2.) Look for steps on the right in around 300m. Turn right up the steps into 'Seabank Road'. Follow the road up to a T junction and turn left.

2. At the end of the straight section of road, immediately before it turns left into 'Park West', bear right onto the Wirral Way. About 150m after you pass beneath the second bridge (Delavor Road Bridge), turn left on the signed 'Banks Road' path. Turn left along the road and follow it over the bridge. At the second road on the left ('Pipers Lane') turn left, then right into 'Bush Way'. Before the end of the cul-de-sac you will see the signed paths into Heswall Dales on the left. Bear left on one of these paths and in around 100m or so, at a junction of footpaths, turn right.

Follow this woodland path—soon with houses and gardens up to the right. Cross a small footbridge and keep ahead on the rising path to eventually exit the woods on a path between gardens to reach a road. Bear right across the road, then, almost immediately, turn left into 'Feather Lane'. This is a short access road with bollards at the end. After the bollards, turn right immediately onto the footpath beside a wall. The path soon swings left and rises. At the top of the rise (before metal railings) turn

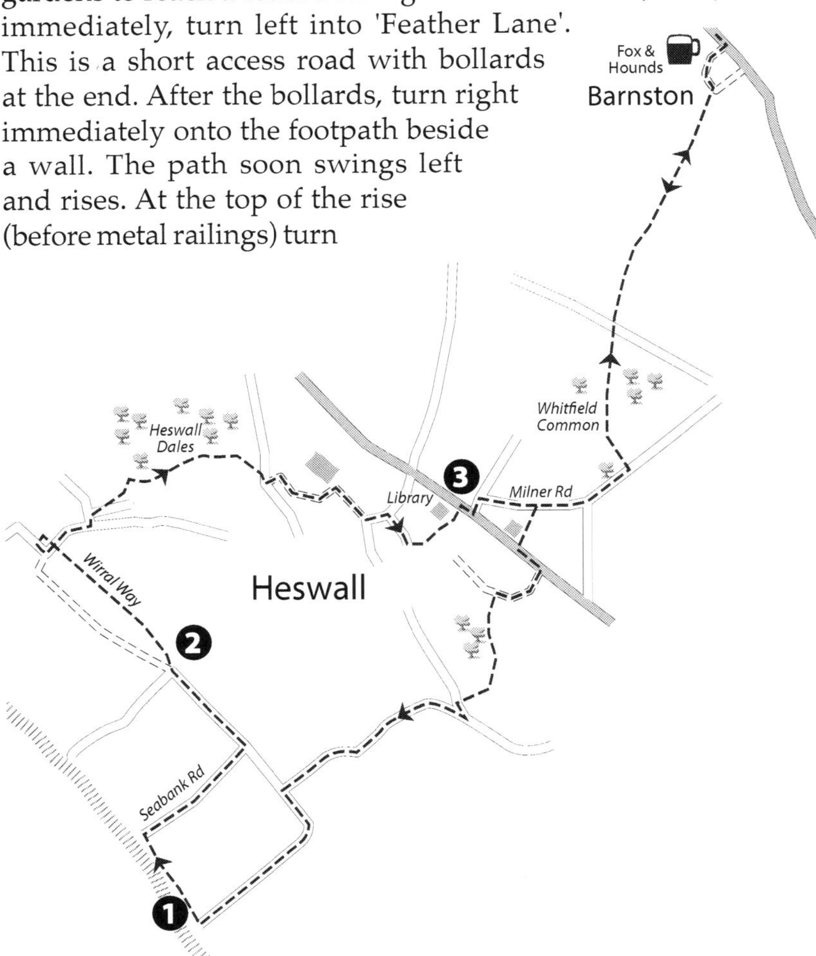

This photograph appears to show the beach known as 'Heswall Shore', now the car park where the walk started

right through the gateway and walk along a rough access road to a T junction at the end.

Turn left here and take the first road on the right: 'Mount Avenue'. Walk up the road keeping left at the 'Jug & Bottle' pub (another good pub). Pass through the car park into Heswall House Gardens and take one of the paths on the left down to the road in the middle of Heswall between Heswall Hall and the Library.

3. Cross the road by the lights and go ahead along 'Downham Road South'. At the end of the shops turn right along 'Milner Road'. Stay on 'Milner Road' until you reach Whitfield Common on the left (shortly after 'Mill Lane' on the right). The access path (Footpath 62) is after house number 117. Don't mistake this for an earlier access into a play area. The path leads into Whitfield Common where there is a three-way path junction. Take the middle path straight ahead. This leads through the now wooded common, crossing a small car park for the sports field and continuing ahead to reach a road close to Heswall Primary School.

Turn left for a few metres then cross over and take the signed footpath ('Barnston') beside the school. Follow the hedged footpath to emerge in fields. This well-used right of way is clearly visible and keeps to field edges at first, then heads directly across the following fields to the small hamlet of Barnston. Pass through a small cemetery to reach a farm track. Turn left along the track, soon between cottages to eventually reach the main road. A left turn here will take you to the **Fox & Hounds**.

From the pub retrace your outward route back across the fields and through Whitfield Common to 'Milner Road'. Turn right along 'Milner Road'.

Just before 'Oban Drive' on the left, take the footpath between gardens also on the left. This emerges in the car park of M&S Foodhall. Go ahead to the road, cross over and turn left. Immediately before the shops on the right, turn right into 'Beacon Lane'.

This lane leads up into a small area of woodland known as The Beacons. Immediately before 'Tower Cottage' bear left into the woods. In around 50m or so take the footpath on the right.

Ignore a right at a fork, then go right at a T junction with houses over to the left. At a gap in the fence and access out of the woods on the left, turn right onto a narrow footpath. This soon opens out into a clearing. Go ahead veering left past a bench dedicated to 'Peter Sparling' and down the bank. The path exits the woods by a narrow enclosed path to emerge onto a driveway (Footpath 9). Go right down the drive and at the road turn left, then right into 'Wall Rake'. At a crossroads go straight ahead along 'Station Road' and at the end of the road turn left at the T junction along 'Riverbank Road'. Follow 'River Bank Road' back to the old beach car park to complete the walk.

Neston Road, Thornton Hough CH64 7TL

Tel: (0151) 353 2920 | **website:** www.brunningandprice.co.uk/redfox/

Brewery: Brunning & Price

Opening times
Monday - Sunday   Noon - 11pm

Meal times
Monday - Thursday   Noon - 9.30pm
Friday & Saturday   Noon - 10pm
Sunday   Noon - 9pm

The pub

Before becoming **The Red Fox** pub, the building was a private residence known by several names over time: 'Westwood', 'Westwood Grange', and later 'The Grange'. It dates back to the mid-19th century and was part of a broader trend in the area, where affluent businessmen purchased plots from the Mostyn Estate to build grand villas either for personal use or rental. The first recorded occupant was James Sawers, a wealthy Liverpool merchant who ran James Sawers & Co., a trading firm with operations in London and South America. Sawers lived there until his business collapsed in 1879, leading to the estate being sold off. The building remained a private residence for many years before being transformed into The Red Fox pub in 2014 by Brunning & Price, preserving its architectural charm while repurposing it for hospitality.

The Red Fox blends period charm with modern elegance, offering gourmet dining and an impressive range of real ales. It's perfect for those who want to pair their walk with a touch of indulgence.

The walk

Distance: 5 miles/8km | **Allow:** 2–2½ hours

Start: Small car park by sports fields in Thornton Hough. No restriction

OS Grid Ref: SJ 303 807 | **What3Words:** along.inner.liability

The route

1. Cross the road and turn right towards the village centre.

Thornton Hough owes much of its present appearance to Lord Leverhulme who practically rebuilt it when he bought nearby Thornton Manor in the 1890s. The neo-Elizabethan style which he chose for Thornton Manor can also be seen in the attractive half-timbered cottages that surround the green. The parish church has the curious distinction of having a five-faced clock and the second church was built by Leverhulme in the Norman style.

Follow the road up to pass the 'Seven Stars' pub and immediately after Thornton Hough Primary School, take the signed

Thornton Hough

footpath ('Public Footpath to Brimstage') on the left. Follow the right of way along an access road to a T junction. Turn right here and in about 60m, turn left onto an enclosed footpath which shortly runs into fields. The path is easily followed through the fields ahead crossing one of the tree-lined driveways to Thornton Manor, home of Lord Leverhulme (over to the left).

Thornton Manor was the home of William Hesketh Lever, the first Viscount Leverhulme, who came to Wirral in 1887 to begin soap manufacture at Port Sunlight. The large Victorian mansion set in beautiful countryside away from the sights and smells of the soap industry obviously appealed to him and he bought the manor outright in 1891. He was a lover of building and in the following years transformed it into the grand Elizabethan-style residence that we see today.

Cross the drive and go through the kissing gate opposite. Walk ahead through two more fields to cross a stile into an enclosed footpath. Ignoring the path to the right, follow the path straight ahead to the road ('Talbot Ave').

2. Turn left at the lane and follow it to a T junction. Go ahead here on the signed fenced path with Thornton Manor on the left. Soon the path passes beneath a footbridge and enters woods and you will get glimpses of a large lake through the trees on your right, part of Thornton Manor estate. Beyond the woods a fenced footpath swings right with a field on the left, before entering woods again. Pass beneath a large pylon and continue ahead through a strip of woodland for about 1km / ½ mile.

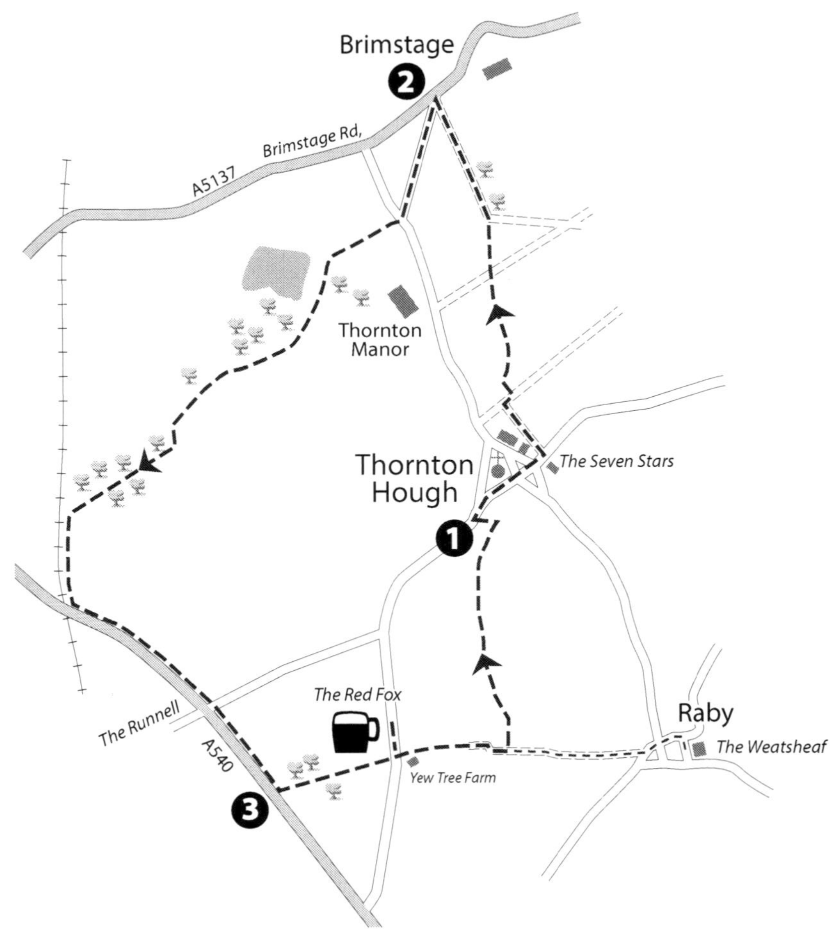

At the end of the wood by the railway, turn left through a kissing gate into a field and walk ahead along the field edge (railway to the right). In the bottom corner of the field bear left again to exit the field in the far corner to reach the main road.

This is the A540 and a short section along this busy highway can not be avoided. It is best to cross over and use the path on the far side. Turn left along the footpath passing houses on the right, then a lane ('The Runnell') also on the right. Continue ahead on the footpath separated from the road by a wide grass verge and trees.

3. In about 500m, look for a signed footpath on the opposite side of the road. Cross the road and follow the path ahead through a strip of woodland to emerge on the B5136.

The Red Fox pub is on your left.

Leaving The Red Fox entrance, turn right along the road and take the signed footpath beside 'Yew Tree Farm' on the left. Follow the enclosed footpath ahead crosssing a footbridge over the stream. At a crossing path, turn left. This is a permissive footpath that heads back towards Thornton Hough (distant church tower visible).

(For a pub with a very different character to The Red Fox, the 'Wheatsheaf Inn' in Raby—the theme for walk 10—makes a good alternative pub for this walk. For this option keep ahead instead of turning left onto the permissive path. Return to this point and turn right to return to Thornton Hough.)

As you get close to the village, go through a gate on the left into the playing fields. A short walk across the green takes you back to the car park to complete the walk.

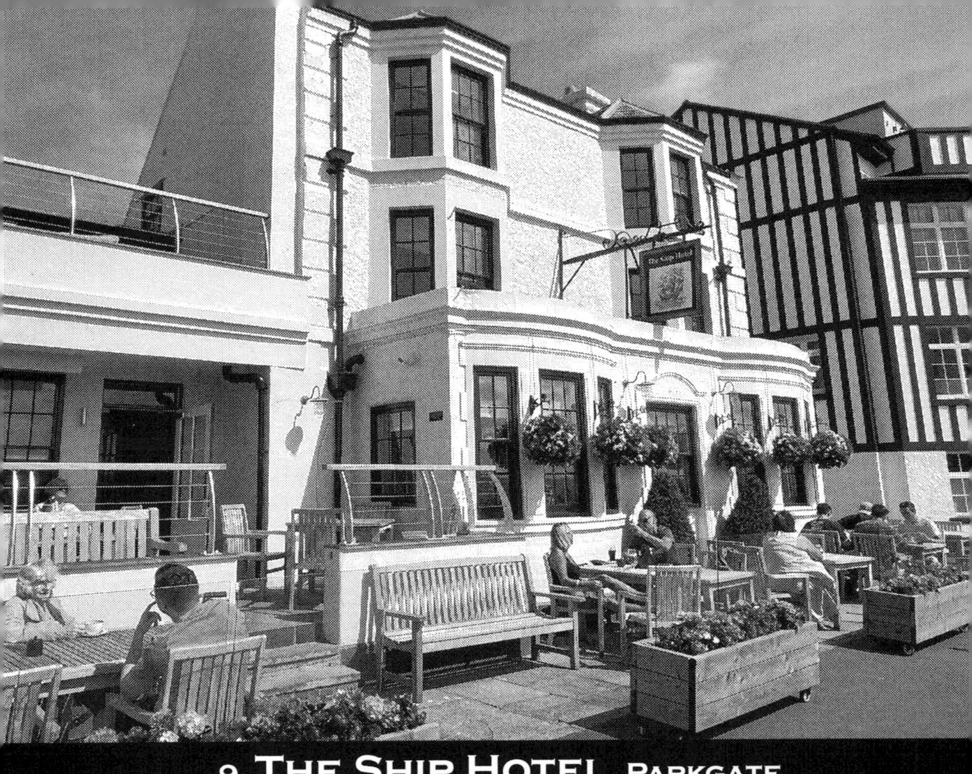

9. THE SHIP HOTEL, PARKGATE

The Parade, Parkgate CH64 6SA

Tel: (0151) 336 3931 | **website:** www.the-shiphotel.co.uk

Brewery: Stange & Co Ltd (www.stangeandco.co.uk)

Opening times
Monday - Sunday   Noon - 11pm

Meal times
Monday - Saturday   Noon - 9pm
Sunday   Noon - 8pm

The pub

The Ship Hotel is an attractive historic coastal inn with roots stretching back to the 18th century. Originally three separate buildings—including a post office and two inns—it was unified and rebuilt in 1859 by the Parkgate Hotel Company, though the venture bankrupted them. Reopened as the Union Hotel in 1860, it later reverted to its original name and became a meeting place for Freemasons until the 1920s.

Today, The Ship Hotel blends maritime heritage with modern comfort. Sympathetically refurbished, it features open fires, a roof-top sun deck with stunning panoramic views over the Dee marshes and a light, airy interior. The pub offers hearty, locally sourced food—especially seafood—along with a strong selection of beers, including its own Portside Pilsner. With 23 en-suite rooms and a welcoming atmosphere, it's a popular retreat for both walkers and diners. Its character lies in its fusion of maritime history, Georgian charm and contemporary hospitality.

The walk

Distance: 4½ miles/7km | **Allow:** 1½-2 hours

Start: Old Baths car park, Parkgate. Free. No time restriction

OS Grid Ref: SJ 274 790 | **What3Words:** exam.lived.sparks

The route

1. From the car park, take the footpath north along the coast (away from Parkgate). The obvious footpath follows the old sandstone seawall with the marshes out to your right all the way to Gayton Cottage where a lane ends right on the marsh edge.

The scant remains beside the car park at the start of the walk are known locally as 'the Old Baths'. The baths were built in 1923 by A.G. Grenfell, headmaster of Mostyn House School, as part of a visionary project to create open-air saltwater swimming pools for both pupils and the public using sea water pumped from the adjacent River Dee.

The baths became a popular destination in the 1920s and 1930s, attracting visitors from across the region. Olympic swimmer Hilda James helped run the site, adding prestige to its reputation.

Unfortunately the baths shared the same fate as Parkgate's once fine sandy beach as the River Dee slowly silted up making water extraction costly. The baths closed during WWII, briefly reopened in 1947, before permanently closing in 1950. The site was later filled in and repurposed as a car park, now a prime spot for birdwatchers overlooking Gayton Marshes.

Turn right and walk up the lane to the T junction.

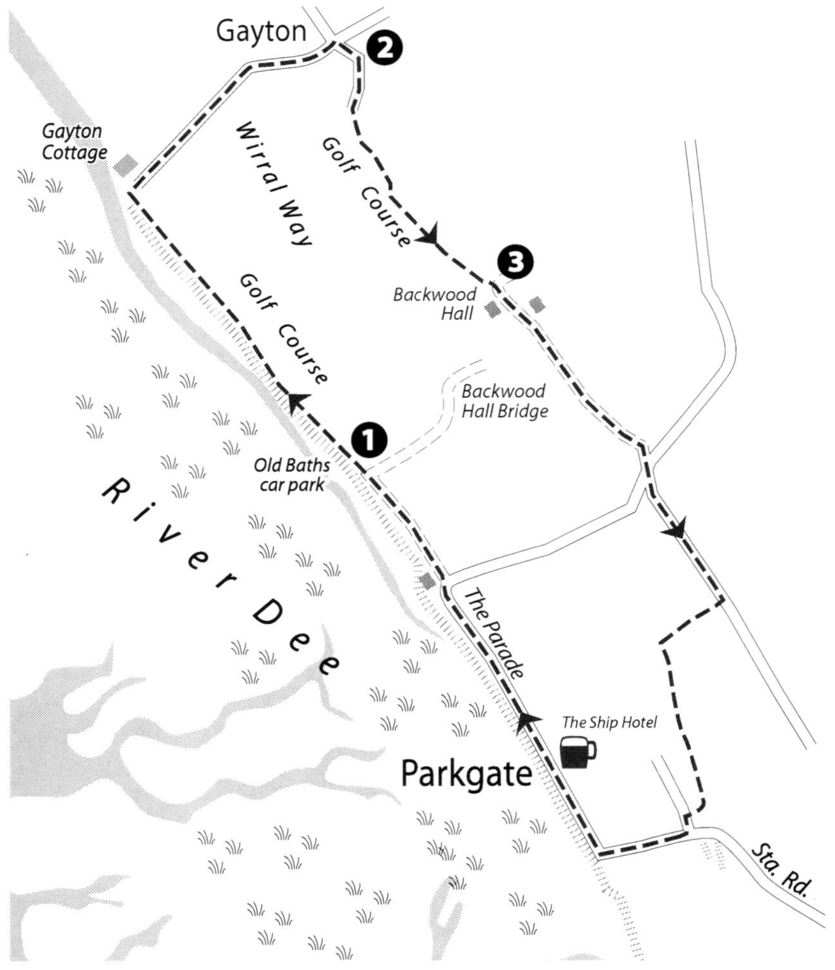

The old sea wall along the marsh edge

2. Turn right here, then right almost immediately into 'Gayton Farm Road' and walk along the old cobbled lane between cottages.

This is the village of Gayton, once a small hamlet but now part of Heswall.

Follow the cobbled lane as it bends right beyond Gayton Hall and soon becomes a rough sunken lane leading onto Heswall Golf Course. The public footpath goes ahead now through a strip of woodland with the golf course to the right. Stay on the footpath ahead ignoring a signed footpath on the right.

At the end of the golf course, a gate leads into fields. The right of way heads directly across the field descending to cross a footbridge over a stream. The path now rises to enter an access road near the buildings of Backwood Hall.

3. Bear left along the road passing between brick gate pillars passing Backwood Hall on the right. Continue along the access road ahead.

At the end of the road go through a kissing gate beside the large metal gate to reach the Parkgate road ('Boathouse Lane'). Cross over and and walk along the lane opposite ('Wood Lane'). Immediately after a small parking area, turn right onto the signed cycleway to 'Neston'. This heads down to join the Wirral Way. Just before the old bridge, bear right up the ramp and turn left over the bridge. Continue along the Wirral Way to where a bridge once spanned the B5135 Pakegate road.

Take the path to the right here to emerge in 'Rope Walk', turning left to reach the B5135. A right turn will now take you down to the old sea front in Parkgate.

A scene from Parkgate's past, probably from the late 1880s or 90s. Lookout for this slipway as you walk along the old sea front back to the car park

A section of Swire & Hutchin's map of Cheshire published in 1829, a time when the River Dee's deep water channel flowed within a stone's throw of the old sea front

Parkgate boasts a rich and layered history shaped by geography, trade and shifting tides—both literal and figurative.

Parkgate's name derives from its location at the gate of Neston's deer hunting park, which dates back to at least 1250. Initially a quiet stretch of marshland, the area began to evolve into a small fishing village thanks to its proximity to the River Dee. As Chester's port became increasingly inaccessible due to silting, Parkgate emerged as a vital maritime alternative.

By the early 18th century, Parkgate had become a significant embarkation point for Ireland. Its strategic location allowed ships to bypass the treacherous channels leading to Chester, making it a preferred stop for merchants and travellers. The town even had its own Customs House, underscoring its importance in trade and migration. Notably, George Frideric Handel returned from Ireland via Parkgate in 1742, and Lady Emma Hamilton, Lord Nelson's mistress, bathed there for health reasons.

Parkgate's fortunes waned as the River Dee continued to silt up, eventually rendering the port unusable. Liverpool, with its deeper waters and growing infrastructure, took over as the region's dominant maritime hub. Parkgate then reinvented itself as a seaside resort in the late 18th century, attracting bathers and day-trippers. However, the encroaching salt marshes—accelerated by the introduction of Sporobolus anglicus grass in 1928—gradually consumed the sandy beaches, diminishing its appeal as a coastal retreat.

Despite its decline as a port, Parkgate retains a distinct charm. Its Georgian architecture, remnants of shipbuilding activity and historical pubs like the Ship Hotel speak of its vibrant past. Today, it's celebrated for its scenic promenade, birdwatching opportunities and famous ice cream parlours—making it a beloved destination for both locals and visitors.

Parkgate's story is one of adaptation: from deer park to port, from resort to quiet village. Its history mirrors the changing tides of commerce, nature and society, leaving behind a legacy etched into the salt marshes and cobbled streets.

The Ship Hotel is the first pub you will come to. After visiting the pub, continue along 'The Parade' to return to the car park and complete the walk.

Raby Mere Road, Raby CH63 4JH

Tel: (0151) 336 3416 | **website:** wheatsheaf-cowshed.co.uk

Brewery: Free House

Opening times

Monday - Saturday	Noon - 11pm
Sunday	Noon - 8pm

Meal times

Monday	Noon - 3.30pm
Tuesday - Saturday	Noon - 8pm
Sunday	Noon - 3.30pm

The pub

The Wheatsheaf Inn in Raby is a cherished gem of Wirral, reputedly the oldest pub on the peninsula, with origins dating back to 1611. Known locally as 'The Thatch' for its distinctive thatched roof and black-and-white timbered façade, it exudes historic charm. The building is Grade II listed and may have served as an inn as early as the 13th century, offering rest to travellers en route to Parkgate and Ireland.

Today, the Wheatsheaf blends tradition with comfort: roaring open fires, oak beams and a converted cattle barn now housing the Cowshed Restaurant. It serves award-winning seasonal dishes and a rotating selection of cask ales, with Brimstage Brewery among its local suppliers. Despite challenges during the pandemic, its loyal patrons braved all weather to support it. With its warm atmosphere, rich history and dedication to quality, The Wheatsheaf Inn remains a cornerstone of Raby's cultural and culinary life.

◆

The walk

Distance: 4¾ miles/7.5km | **Allow:** 1–1½ hours

Start: Wirral Country Park car park in Lees Lane, Neston. No restriction

OS Grid Ref: SJ 306 775 | **What3Words:** nibbled.names.graph

The route

1. Return to the car park entrance and turn right along the lane. At the main road turn left and at 'Hinderton Mount Residential Home', cross the busy main road and the stile opposite into a large field. Go ahead through the field and at the end of the path turn right along the lane. In around 10m or so, turn left into 'School Lane'. The lane soom becomes little more than a farm road between Hinderton Hall and farmland.

Hinderton Hall is a Grade II listed building built in 1856 for Liverpool wine merchant Christopher Bushell. Designed by Alfred Waterhouse—later famed for the Natural History Museum—it's one of his earliest works. Constructed in sandstone with steep slate roofs and a distinctive tower, the hall reflects Gothic Revival architecture. Over the years, it's served various roles, including offices and event space,

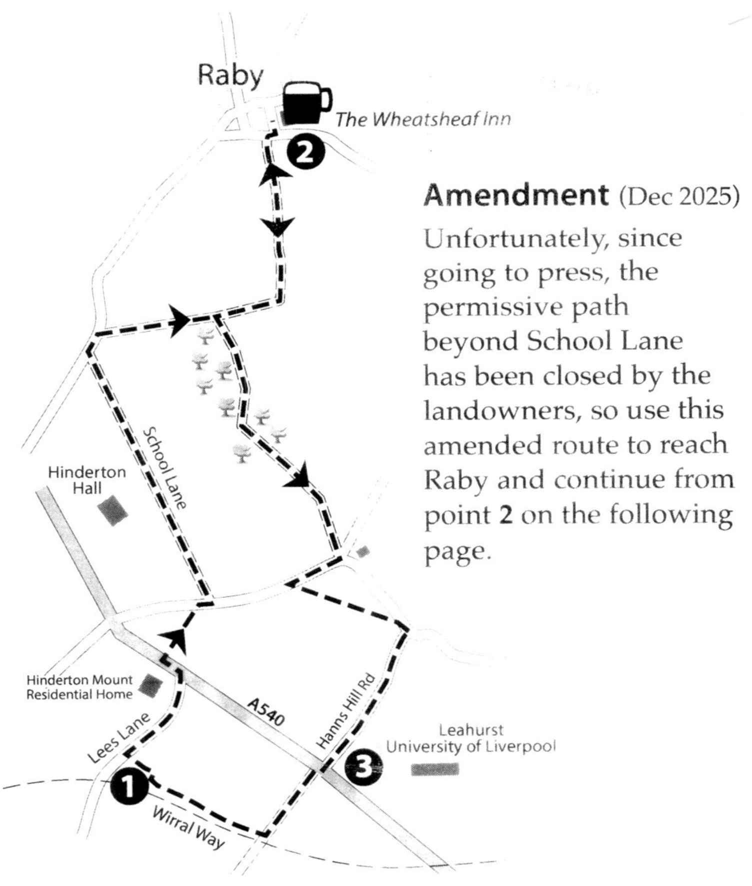

Amendment (Dec 2025)

Unfortunately, since going to press, the permissive path beyond School Lane has been closed by the landowners, so use this amended route to reach Raby and continue from point **2** on the following page.

but is now a private residence. The estate includes lodges, cottages and landscaped gardens across three acres.

At the end of 'School Lane' turn right along the road for around 30m. Turn right here (immediately after 'The Field House') onto the signed footpath, which, beyound a large gate, continues between hedges to eventually reach a footpath T juntion. Turn left and follow the path between hedged fields to reach a lane beside 'Jasmine Cottage'. **The Wheatsheaf Inn** is directly ahead.

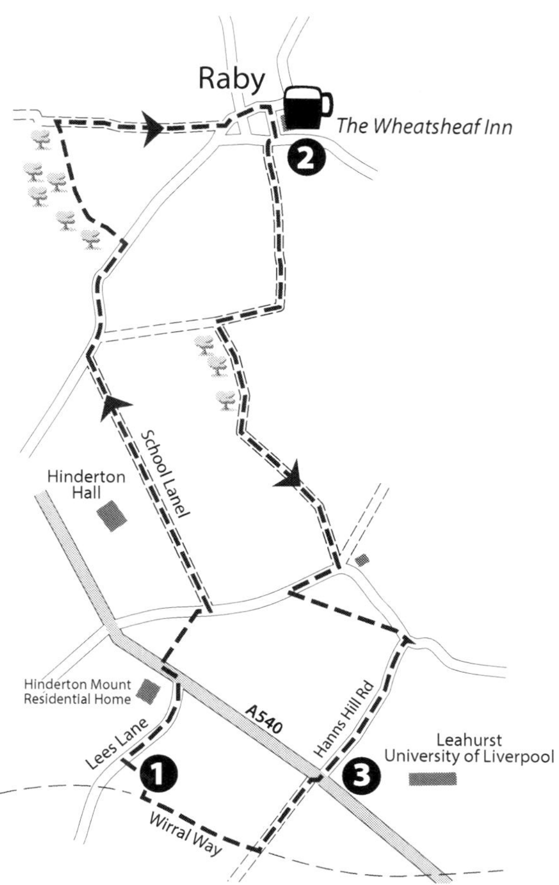

but is now a private residence. The estate includes lodges, cottages and landscaped gardens across three acres.

At the end of 'School Lane' turn right and walk along the road for around 400m. At the Wirral Borough boundary sign look for a signed permissive path on the left. The path is fenced and passes between fields at first, then beside woods on the left.

At a junction of paths turn right and follow a good, hedged footpath between hedges to emerge on 'Raby Road' on the edge of Raby.

Bear left along the road and take the second lane on the right ('The Green') where you will find **The Wheatsheaf Inn**.

2. Leaving the pub, go left along the lane. At a T junction go straight ahead here past 'Jasamine Cottage' on the right and through a kissing gate onto a broad farm track. Where the track enters fields ahead, turn right through a kissing gate onto a footpath between hedges. At a junction of paths on the edge of woods and below power cables, turn left. This path follows a strip of old woodland between farmland for about 1km/¾ mile.

At the end of the path turn right and walk along the road (the road is quite busy but there is a grass verge for much of the way). Look for a signed footpath on the left. Turn left over the stile and follow the path ahead through fields to a driveway. Turn right then right almost immediately along 'Quarry Lane'. At the road junction go right along 'Hanns Hall Road'. Follow the road up to the main A 540. The road can be busy but there is a footpath all the way.

3. At the main road cross over with care and take the farm road directly opposite (Cuckoo Lane). At the Wirral Way turn right back into the car park to complete the walk.

19 Quayside, Little Neston CH64 0TB

Tel: (0151) 336 6980 | **website:** theharpinn.com

Brewery: Admiral Taverns

Opening times

Monday - Thursday	Noon - 11pm
Friday & Saturday	Noon - 11.30pm
Sunday	Noon - 11pm

Meal times

Monday	Noon - 3pm
Tuesday	Noon - 8pm, 5pm - 7.30pm
Wednesday - Sunday	Noon - 3pm

The pub

The **Harp Inn** is a cozy 'locals' style pub nestled on the banks of the Dee Estuary on the King Charles III England Coast Path and Dee Marshes Cycle Route, with wide open views across to

North Wales. Recently refurbished with investment from Admiral Taverns and licensee Julie Woolley, the pub now boasts a more welcoming interior, historic photos, and a revamped beer garden. Known for its traditional pub food—like steak and Guinness pie, fish and chips and the Harp's signature burger, and its mix of regular and rotating local ales—it's a popular spot for both locals and visitors.

The pub has a rich and layered history that stretches back to the 18th century when it would have looked out across the vast tidal waters of the River Dee. Originally built as three cottages around 1750, two of them were converted into a pub in 1780 and named *'Hay House'*. By the 1820s, it was known as the *'Welsh Harp'*, and later served as a local hub for coal miners working at nearby Neston Colliery, which closed in 1927. It adopted its current name, *Harp Inn*, around 1856.

The walk

Distance: 6½ miles/10.5km | **Allow:** 2–2½ hours

Start: Free parking in a layby near the junction of Station Road and Denhall Lane, Burton. No time restriction

OS Grid Ref: SJ 301 747 | **What3Words:** example.weekends.sideburns

The route

1. From the layby turn right (when facing the marshes) along the road. Where the road turns right away from the marshes, take the private road ahead. This leads along the edge of the marshes and what, as recently as 150 years ago, would have been the coastline (see the map of the following page), passing Net's Café and Denhall House Farm.

The lane soon becomes a much narrower tarmac cycleway (now part of the new King Charles III England Coast Path). As you approach houses ahead look for a footpath on the right. Turn right here and follow the path as it runs between houses on the left and fields on the right. Ignore a path on the left keeping ahead to eventually join an unsurfaced farm road. Follow the road under the railway to reach a lane. Turn right and follow the lane (Well Lane) into the village of Ness.

At the T junction, turn sharp left passing 'The Wheatsheaf' pub. Within a few metres cross the road and turn right down 'Cumbers Lane'. At the end of the lane, by 'Sunny View' take the footpath directly ahead entering fields by a kissing gate. The path curves leftwards through a large open field to a kissing gate. Go through the kissing gate and past the play area.

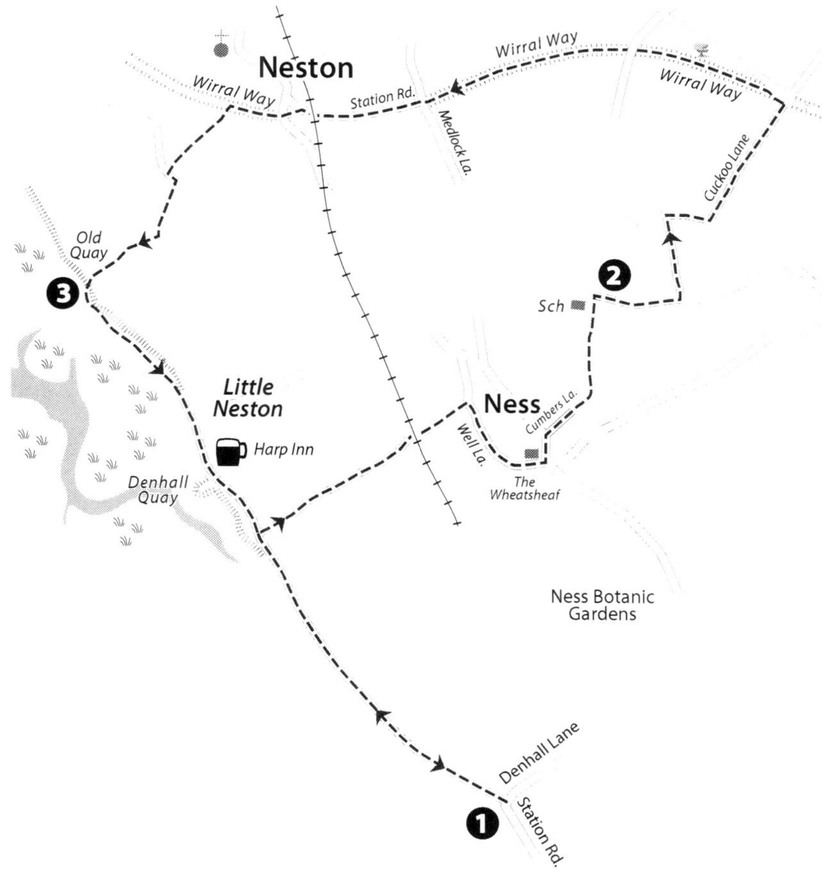

A section of Swire & Hutchin's map of Cheshire, published in 1829 showing the dramatic changes that have occurred along the coastline

2. At the road beside 'Woodfall Primary School', turn right. Don't follow the road as it swings left in a few metres to join 'Gorstons Lane', instead, take the hedged bridleway ahead. In around 300m turn left along a signed footpath. Like the bridleway, this path is hedged but much narrower.

At a footpath junction take the fenced footpath ahead and at the T junction at the end of the path, turn right. Follow this footpath between fields to join a broad sunken lane at a T junction. Turn left here and follow the old lane—worn down below the level of the surrounding fields. One of many old lanes which never became formalised into tarmac roads.

Immediately before the old railway bridge now carrying the Wirral Way, turn left through a footgate and up steps to reach the old trackbed. Turn left along the Wirral Way.

The Wirral Way is a walking and cycling trail following the line of the old Birkenhead Railway, which ran between West Kirby and Hooton and opened in 1866. Passenger services ceased in 1956 and the line closed in 1962. The bed of the railway was renovated and the Wirral Way opened in 1973. It has been a popular traffic-free route for walkers, cyclists and horose riders for over 50 years.

Beyond Lees Lane bridge the Wirral Way runs through a rock cutting to eventually emerge close the the centre of Neston. The next section of the old trackbed has been lost to modern housing development, so cross the road and go ahead along 'Station Road'.

At the end of 'Station Road' pass under the railway bridge and look for the access to the Wirral Way on the left by the car park. Turn left along the Wirral Way shortly crossing the bridge over the road. Around 200m after crossing the bridge, there is a junction of paths—turn left here on the signed footpath to the 'Old Quay'. Go through the kissing gate and shortly enter an open field. Keep along the right-hand field edge to pass through

The remains of Denhall Quay near the Harp Inn

Remains of the sandstone quay now look out onto miles of saltmarsh

a gap in the far corner beneath power lines. Cross a small field to reach a footpath contained between hedges.

Turn left along the path, soon entering fields again. The footpath ahead is gravel surfaced and heads across more fields to reach the site of the 'Old Quay'; the remains of an Elizabethan sea port. Bear to the right here over a footbridge to see the remains of old sandstone quay.

It's hard to imagine that these scant remains were once a bustling sandstone quay and ancient port, vital to regional trade. The flat open field around the footbridge was at one time a small inlet and is thought to be the location of 'Lightfoot's Pool', where a small brook flowed into the River Dee—a site already in use as a sheltered anchorage away from the open estuary.

In the 16th century, as the River Dee silted and Chester's port struggled to accommodate sea-going vessels, the port that was established here emerged as a vital lifeline. Constructed with timber from royal forests, local sandstone and civic investment, it served as a satellite dock for Chester, allowing goods like wine, cloth and hides to reach the city via smaller boats.

The quay was part of a broader effort to maintain Chester's trading prominence. Though short-lived, its role was crucial during a transitional period in regional commerce. As silting worsened, trade moved further downstream to Parkgate and eventually to Liverpool, which rose to dominate maritime trade by the 19th century.

Today, the weathered stones of the Old Quay and the nearby Old Quay House (used as a customs house) offer a glimpse into this forgotten chapter. They stand as quiet reminders of Neston's brief but ambitious attempt to anchor itself in the shifting tides of history.

3. Head back across the footbridge and follow the path ahead to cross the sandstone wall by steps.

The stone work here is the site of the Old Quay House.

The path ahead follows the old river bank and has recently been improved as part of the push to formalise this section of the King Charles III England Coast Path. At 'Quayside' road, go ahead along the road to eventually reach the **Harp Inn**.

To complete the walk follow the road beyond the Harp Inn which joins the path and cycleway along the marsh edge used earlier.

Beyond the Harp Inn, but before you join the cycleway, you will see a line of sandstone blocks on your right—these are the remains of Denhall Quay (photo on page 71) which served the nearby Ness Colliery and is thought to have been built around 1790. Period photos from the early 1900s show 6-8 lines of blocks which now lie buried by silting of the river, leaving only the top row to look out over acres of marsh grass where there was once deep water.

13. THE MAGAZINE, WALLASEY

7 Magazine Brow, New Brighton, Wallasey CH45 1HP

Tel: (0151) 630 3169 | **website:** the-magazine-hotel.co.uk

Brewery: Bass

Opening times

Monday - Saturday	12.30noon - 11.30pm
Sunday	11.30am - 11.00pm

Meal times

Monday - Thursday	12noon - 3pm

The pub

The Magazine is a cherished local institution steeped in history and character. Established in 1759, it stands proudly within the Magazines Conservation Area, offering panoramic views of the River Mersey and the Liverpool waterfront. Inside, the pub retains its original charm with cosy snugs, open fireplaces and a warm, welcoming atmosphere. Known for its exceptional cask ales—including the rare draught Bass and local favourites like Brimstage's Trapper's Hat—it's a haven for beer enthusiasts.

The Magazine also hosts regular live music, folk nights and a popular weekly quiz, reinforcing its role as a vibrant community hub. Its spacious beer garden is a favourite in warmer months, while the interior offers comfort and tradition year-round.

◆

The walk

Distance: 3¾ miles/6km | **Allow:** 1–1½ hours

Start: There is plenty of parking available on the sea front in the approach to New Brighton. No time restriction at the time of writing.

OS Grid Ref: SJ298 941 | **What3Words:** exchanges.lazy.sooner

The route

1. Head towards the centre of New Brighton along the sea front. Walk with the Marine Point Retail Park on your right and the sea on the left ('Ian Fraser Walk'). Continue beside the marine lake towards Fort Perch Rock with the lighthouse over to the left set against the giant cranes at the Liverpool container port.

Fort Perch Rock, like many other forts around Britain's coast, was built between 1825 and 1829 to defend the Port of Liverpool from potential French invasion during the Napoleonic Wars. Designed by Captain John Sikes Kitson of the Royal Engineers, it stands on a sandstone reef known as Black Rock and was nicknamed the "Little Gibraltar of the Mersey" for its formidable sandstone walls and 18 guns.

Though it looked ready for battle, the fort never saw any real combat. Decommissioned in 1956, it has had a number of uses including a museum and cultural venue, hosting concerts, exhibitions and even escape rooms. It remains a Grade II listed building and is a notable landmark from New Brighton's maritime heritage.*

At the fort access ramp at the end of the lake, bear right towards the Floral Pavillion. Continue along the sea front which soon becomes 'Tower Promenade' passing 'Pier House'—both names recalling former landmarks.

New Brighton Tower, built between 1898 and 1900, once stood as Britain's tallest structure at 567 feet. It was designed to rival Blackpool Tower and featured a ballroom, theatre and leisure grounds. The site was a little further along the sea front at what is now known as 'The Tower Grounds'. Despite its prominence and undoubted popularity it fell into disuse during World War I and, a little over 20 years after it was built, was dismantled for scrap by 1921. Its base, the Tower Ballroom, remained a cultural hub until fire destroyed it in 1969. There are no signs of the tower or the associated buildings today.

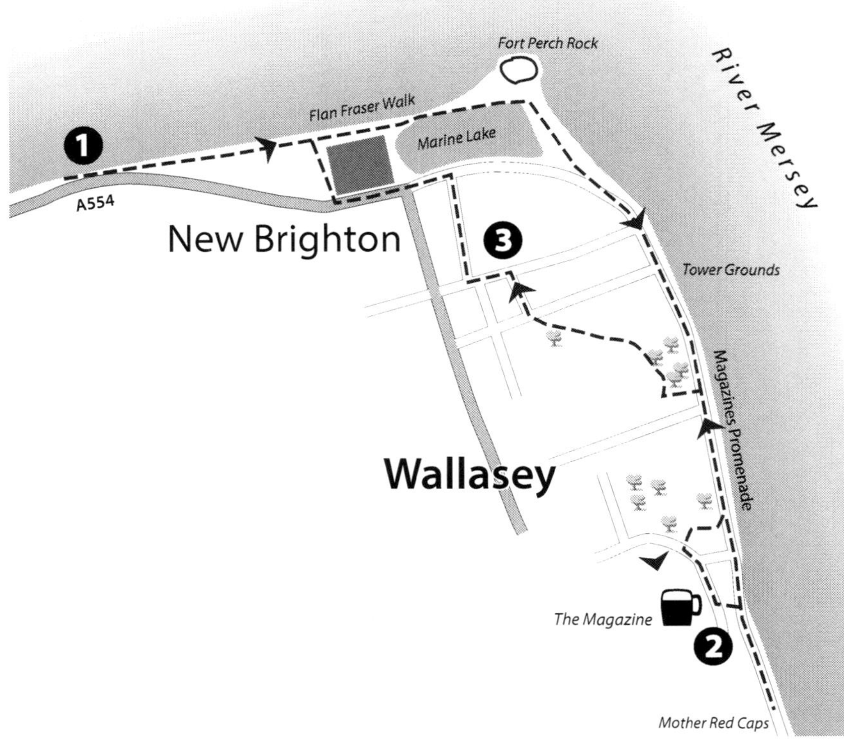

Fort Perch Rock and the Llighthouse

New Brighton Pier—which stood just across the road from the Tower—was an earlier landmark, designed by Eugenius Birch and opened in 1867. It was a 600-foot iron structure offering saloons, refreshment rooms and views of the Mersey and Liverpool waterfront. It was a well known and well-loved seaside attraction, evolving through the decades with pavilions and entertainment. Despite efforts to preserve it, structural decline led to its closure in 1972 and demolition by 1982. Today, it lives only in memory and rare photographs.

Continue along the 'Magazines Promenade'. You can enjoy views across the river and even wander down onto the sections of beach from here. You will shortly see 'The Magazine' pub up to the right, but it is worth continuing a little further if you have time. The mainly pedestrian road continues all the way to Seacombe Ferry. Retrace your steps to here for The Magazine pub.

Just beyond the modern-day Mother Redcap's Care Home, visitors will spot a charming whitewashed cottage adorned with a mural that pays tribute to one of Wallasey's most legendary figures. The mural commemorates Mother Redcap and the infamous tavern she once ran—a place steeped in maritime lore dating back to the late 1500s.

Named for her striking red hood, Mother Redcap was reputed to have aided smugglers, turning her tavern into a refuge for sailors, rogues and adventurers along the Mersey. With its thick stone walls, trapdoors and hidden cellars, the pub became the stuff of legend—whispers of secret tunnels and stashed contraband filled the air. Locals even claimed she safeguarded prize money and illicit goods, earning her the nickname of Wallasey's first banker.

Though the original building was demolished in 1974, its spirit lives on. Today, Mother Redcap remains a symbol of coastal cunning, community folklore and the romantic shadow of England's smuggling heritage.

2. Leaving the pub, turn left along the street, soon passing 'The Pilot Boat' pub over to the left.

There are a few cottages here that have clearly been around for some time and were part of a tiny fishing community at one time. Soon you will pass an impressive sandstone gatehouse looking a bit out of place.

This impressive gatehouse comes as a bit of a surprise in this location. It formed the entrance to a walled enclosure known as 'The Magazines', originally built in 1751 in what was then a secluded riverside site. It was used for storing gunpowder and ordnance from ships entering the port of Liverpool as a safely measure. By 1858, it had evolved into Liscard Battery, built to defend the Mersey, when the castellated gateway you can see today was added. Nearby cottages, originally the homes of fishermen, later housed artillery officers, forming a unique maritime and military heritage.

Immediately after the gatehouse cross the cobbled street and enter 'Vale Park' on the right with its unusual collection of carvings. Bear right through the park and exit back onto 'The Magazines Promenade'. Turn left.

Immediately after 'Dolmorton Road' (second road on the

The slightly out-of-place looking gatehouse to The Magazines

left) turn left into a small area of woodland, following a narrow footpath up a series of steps. Before you reach the upper edge of the woods, bear right onto a footpath which soon opens out into playing fields occupying the site of the former New Brighton Tower. Walk ahead through the playing fields keeping to the left to exit in the far left corner onto 'Egerton Street'. Cross the street and go ahead along 'Mason Street'.

Various art murals decorate the surrounding buildings with themes from The Beatles to the ship created from driftwood that once stood on the nearby beach.

At the T junction, cross over and turn left along Victoria Road soon passing the excellent Bowlegged Beagle micro pub and bar. Continue to the end of the road and at the traffic lights turn right. Follow the road down to the roundabout beside the Marine Point Retail Park again. Cross over, and head back through the retail park to complete the walk.

14. THE TAP, EASTHAM FERRY

Ferry Road, Eastham CH62 0AU

Tel: (0151) 328 1648 | **website**: www.tapeastham.co.uk

Brewery: Marston's

Opening times

Monday - Thursday	11.30am - Midnight
Friday & Saturday	11.30am - 00.30am
Sunday	11.30am - Midnight

Meal times

| Monday - Sunday | 11.30am - 4pm |

The pub

The Tap at Eastham Ferry is an attractive riverside pub steeped in history, dating back to 1745. Originally known as the *Tap Room*, it has worn many names over the centuries, including *Eastham Vaults* and *Pier Bar*. Today, it's a welcoming spot with traditional decor, roaring log fires and stunning views across the River Mersey to the distant Liverpool skyline. Popular with bikers, dog walkers and locals alike, it offers a cosy atmosphere and a rotating selection of Marston's ales.

Situated beside Eastham Country Park and the old ferry pier, it provides a perfect stop for lunch and drinks at the end of a short and easy walk in Eastham Woods.

The walk

Distance: 2 miles/3.25km | **Allow:** 1 hour

Start: Car park for Eastham Country Park, Ferry Road, Eastham

OS Grid Ref: SJ 363 818 | **What3Words:** lofts.dart.vase

The route

1. Walk out of the car park entrance and at the mini roundabout turn left along the road passing through a series of parking areas. At the end of the road a footpath continues ahead with the river beyond railings on the right. A little further on is the site of Job's Ferry, where steps beyond a gate in the railings lead down to the shore where there are sandstone blocks.

Job's Ferry is one of the earliest known ferry services across the River Mersey. It predates Eastham Ferry and dates back to the 1300s. Operated by monks from the Abbey of St. Werburgh in Chester, Job's Ferry connected Eastham to Liverpool long before modern transport links existed.

While Eastham Ferry officially began in 1509, Job's Ferry was slightly further north and served as a vital crossing point during the Middle Ages. These early ferries were powered by sail and oar, and, depending on river conditions, the journey could take hours. Eventually, paddle steamers replaced sailboats in the 19th century, but the rise of railways led to the decline of ferry services.

Eventually a gate in the railings ahead leads out of the country park. For a view across the river to the Liverpool skyline go through the gate and ahead for a few hundred metres to a raised concrete area.

Retrace your steps back into the country park woodland passing through the gate again. Turn right immediately after the gate onto a sandy rising footpath that soon swings left to a clearing with benches and a meeting of paths. Turn right here onto a footpath which soon runs beside railings on the right on the edge of the woods.

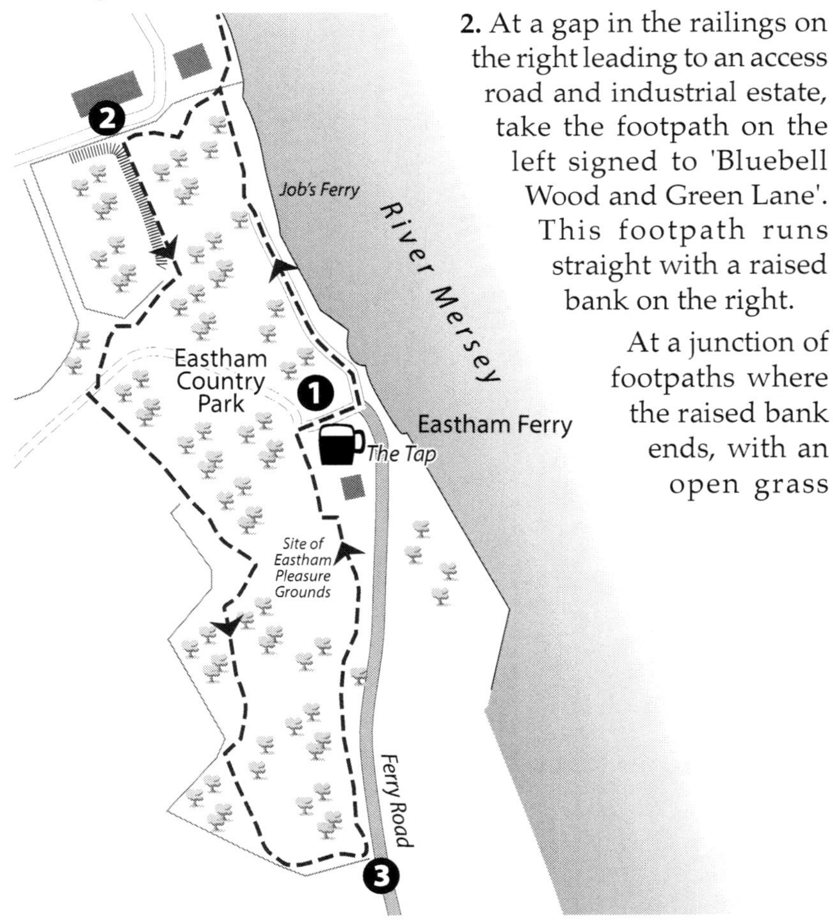

2. At a gap in the railings on the right leading to an access road and industrial estate, take the footpath on the left signed to 'Bluebell Wood and Green Lane'. This footpath runs straight with a raised bank on the right.

At a junction of footpaths where the raised bank ends, with an open grass

Looking across the River Mersey from the old Eastham Ferry pier

area visible through the trees ahead and left, turn right. At the next crosspaths junction in around 130m with a large concrete block on the right, keep ahead on a footpath beside a fence.

The next junction is with a very broad crossing path (Bluebell information panel on the right). Turn right here and in around 20m, immediately before an open field, turn left onto a narrower footpath. The field will now visible through the trees on the right). At the end of the field there is a gap in the trees—continue ahead for around 120m, before turning right onto a well established footpath signed to 'Beech Wood'.

Follow the footpath through the woods—a grove of mature beech trees, many sadly felled by recent gales, although there are young saplings too.

The path eventually swings left around the edge of the woods. Stay on the path swinging left again when you reach the edge of the woods near Ferry Road (the lane used to access the country park). The footpath stays close to the edge of the woods parallel to the lane on the right.

At a clearing, the path forks. For a quick return to 'The Tap' keep ahead—to continue the walk and return to the car park, bear left and at a T junction turn left. This path passes through the area once occupied by the Pleasure Gardens. Within a few metres you will see various remains on the left.

Eastham Pleasure Gardens, created in the mid-1800s, were a vibrant Victorian attraction. Landscaped with ornamental trees and fountains, they featured a zoo, ballroom, bandstand and rollercoaster. Thousands visited for music, performances and even a swimming elephant stunt. The grand Jubilee Arch welcomed guests, while the gardens offered both spectacle and serenity. Though they declined by the 1930s, remnants like the bear pit and fountains remain, echoing a rich legacy of leisure and entertainment.

Return a few metres to the main footpath bearing left as indicated by the 'Visitor Centre, Information and Toilets' sign. The area to the left of the path here is the site of the curious Bear Pit.

The Bear Pit is a haunting remnant of Eastham's Victorian heyday. Built in the 1870s, the bear pit was part of a larger attraction designed to draw visitors from Liverpool and beyond via paddle steamer ferries. The pit itself was a sunken, circular enclosure made of stone, where two brown bears were kept for public entertainment. It was surrounded by railings so visitors could peer down into the enclosure. Alongside the bear pit, the gardens also featured monkey cages, an aviary, lions, camels and even circus performances.

The bear pit sat near a bandstand and stage area where entertainers performed. Though now derelict, you can still trace the outlines of these features, offering a surreal window into a time when exotic animals were part of leisure culture.

Continue ahead to reach the car park to complete the walk.

Mara Books

Mara Books publish a range of walking books for Cheshire and North Wales and have the following list to date. A complete list of current titles is available on our web site: www.northerneyebooks.co.uk

Cheshire
Leisure walks series

Short walks from Wirral villages
ISBN 978-1-902512-23-5. A collection of 30 short walks designed with the less able walker in mind with distances ranging from just 1 mile to a maximum of 4¾ miles.

Circular Walks in Wirral
ISBN 978-1-902512-21-1. A collection of circular walks in the coast and countryside of Wirral.

Walks in Mysterious Cheshire and Wirral
ISBN 978-1-902512-60-0. Second edition. A collection of themed circular walks exploring Cheshire's historic landscape.

Walks in West Cheshire and Wirral
ISBN 978-1-902512-36-5. Thirty of the best walks to be enjoyed in west Cheshire and Wirral.

Circular walks along the Sandstone Trail
ISBN 978-1-902512-10-5. A well established title, now in its fifth edition, featuring 13 linked circular walks ranged along the popular Sandstone Trail.

Walking Cheshire's Sandstone Trail
ISBN 978-1-908632-01-2. The official guide to Cheshire's premier walking route. The trail is described in detail and is illustrated with full colour photographs and Ordnance Survey mapping.

Best Pub Walks in Cheshire
ISBN 978-1-902512-32-7. A collection of 30 superb walks to some of the best country pubs in Cheshire.

North Wales

Leisure walks series

Coastal Walks around Anglesey

ISBN 978-1-902512-20-4. A collection of circular walks which explore the varied scenery of Anglesey's beautiful coastline.

Walking on the Lleyn Peninsula

ISBN 978-1-902512-00-6. A collection of circular walks exploring the wild and beautiful coastline and hills of the Lleyn Peninsula.

Circular Walks in the Conwy Valley

ISBN 978-0-9522409-7-6. A collection of circular walks which explore the varied scenery of this beautiful valley, from the Great Orme to Betws-y-Coed.

Walking in Northern Snowdonia

ISBN 978-1-902512-06-8. Twenty of the best low-level walks in northern half of the Snowdonia National Park.

Walking in the Clwydian Range

ISBN 978-1-902512-14-3. A collection of 21 circular walks exploring the Clwydian Range Area of Outstanding Natural Beauty (AONB).

Best Walks in North Wales

ISBN 978-1-902512-37-2. A collection of 21 of the very best circular walks ranged throughout North Wales, from the wilds of the Lleyn Peninsula through Anglesey and Snowdonia to the rolling hills of the Clwydian Range.